Student Handbook
for

FUNDAMENTAL STATISTICS
for the
BEHAVIORAL SCIENCES

Third Edition

David C. Howell

University of Vermont

Duxbury Press
An Imprint of Wadsworth Publishing Company
I(T)P™ An International Thomson Publishing Company

Belmont • Albany • Bonn • Boston • Cincinnati • Detroit • London
Madrid • Melbourne • Mexico City • New York • Paris • San Francisco
Singapore • Tokyo • Toronto • Washington

For more information, contact Wadsworth Publishing Company.

Wadsworth Publishing Company
10 Davis Drive
Belmont, California 94002
USA

International Thomson Editores
Campos Eliseos 385, Piso 7
Col. Polanco
11560 México D.F. México

International Thomson Publishing Europe
Berkshire House 168-173
High Holborn
London, WC1V 7AA
England

International Thomson Publishing GmbH
Königswinterer Strasse 418
53227 Bonn
Germany

Thomas Nelson Australia
102 Dodds Street
South Melbourne 3205
Victoria, Australia

International Thomson Publishing Asia
221 Henderson Road
#05-10 Henderson Building
Singapore 0315

Nelson Canada
1120 Birchmount Road
Scarborough, Ontario
Canada M1K 5G4

International Thomson Publishing Japan
Hirakawacho Kyowa Building, 3F
2-2-1 Hirakawacho
Chiyoda-ku, Tokyo 102
Japan

Printer: Malloy Lithographing, Inc.

ISBN 0-534-23980-3 (Student Handbook)
ISBN 0-534-23981-1 (Student Handbook with Macintosh disk)
ISBN 0-534-23978-1 (Student Handbook with MS-DOS disk)

Table of Contents

Page

Preface
Part I: Data Analyses Using StataQuest 1
Part II: Student Solutions Manual with Hints and Suggestions 43
Solutions for Chapter 1   Introduction 45
Solutions for Chapter 2   Basic Concepts 47
Solutions for Chapter 3   Displaying Data 50
Solutions for Chapter 4   Central Tendency 54
Solutions for Chapter 5   Measures of Variability 56
Solutions for Chapter 6   Normal Distribution 60
Solutions for Chapter 7   Probability 68
Solutions for Chapter 8   Hypothesis Testing 71
Solutions for Chapter 9   Correlation 74
Solutions for Chapter 10   Regression 83
Solutions for Chapter 11   Multiple Regression 88
Solutions for Chapter 12   One-Sample t Test 90
Solutions for Chapter 13   Related-Samples t Test 94
Solutions for Chapter 14 t for Two Independent Samples 98
Solutions for Chapter 15   Power 105
Solutions for Chapter 16   One-way ANOVA 112
Solutions for Chapter 17   Factorial ANOVA 124
Solutions for Chapter 18   Repeated Measures ANOVA 132
Solutions for Chapter 19   Chi-Square 138
Solutions for Chapter 20   Distribution-free Tests 144
Solutions for Chapter 21   Choosing the Appropriate Analysis . 151

Preface

This manual serves two distinct purposes. The first part is an introduction to a good-quality, easy-to-use, and inexpensive statistical package called StataQuest, to be used in conjunction with the main text, *Fundamentals of Statistics for the Behavioral Sciences (3rd edition),* to increase your understanding of statistical procedures. More about that shortly. The second part contains more extensive answers to many of the exercises in the text than could be included in an appendix to that book. Both of these sections are intended to help you learn more about basic statistical procedures.

STATAQUEST SOFTWARE

Computer software is changing the way we do many things in life, and in particular the teaching and learning of statistics. The use of statistical software opens opportunities that were not practical when we did everything on a calculator. For example, we can quickly plot data, isolate extreme values, and investigate what happens to standard analyses when we include, or omit, extreme values or special subgroups of subjects.

The StataQuest software that is available with *Fundamental Statistics for the Behavioral Sciences (3rd edition)* will perform nearly all of the analyses described in the text. The software has an easy-to-use menu structure, and produces excellent graphics and clear analysis tables. The purpose of Part I of this manual is to introduce students to that software.

It was not my intent to write an exhaustive manual on StataQuest. My purpose was to lead you through basic analyses with interesting data so that you gain a sense of how to proceed. From there you can work things out for yourself from the menus and the "help" functions. In my experience, a small jump start is really all that is needed. I have included several sections on basic operations, including a discussion of how to read and edit data. These sections were taken with only minor revisions from material prepared by Anagnoson and DeLeon.[1]

---

[1] Anagnoson, J. T., and DeLeon, R. E. (1994) *StataQuest*; (1994) *StataQuest Text Companion.* Belmont, CA, Wadsworth/Duxbury.

StataQuest is available in both DOS and Macintosh formats. The commands are exactly the same, as is the output. The only real difference, aside from whether or not you use a mouse, is in how you install and start the program, and there are separate sections on doing that.

I hope that students will experiment with StataQuest and work through many of the examples and exercises in the text. That is the best way I know to come to understand what statistical analyses are all about. I encourage my students to play with data, to alter them and see what happens, to perform several different analyses on the same data and compare the results, and to do any other thing that they can think of. You don't have to run the analyses I run. Try other approaches. Some of those will turn out not to work at all, or to be silly, but you will learn a very great deal in the process. If students or instructors find particularly interesting things in the process, I would enjoy hearing about them. I can be reached either via the U.S. Postal Service, or by the Internet at David.Howell@uvm.edu.

SOLUTIONS TO EXERCISES

In addition to describing the use of StataQuest, this manual is a guide in helping you to learn statistics through experience solving problems. It includes complete answers to approximately half of the homework exercises given in the main text. These are the same questions for which answers are provided in the back of that book, but the answers here are far more elaborate and instructive. For each exercise I included a hint on how to go about solving the problem, or an interpretation of the result, or some understanding of how the problem fits with what you are trying to learn. An exercise is more than doing the arithmetic, and I have worked to make the answers more than the arithmetic. The more I teach, and the more material I learn on my own, the more I have come to believe that you will not learn statistics (or any other subject matter) simply by reading the book. You have to be involved in doing something with the material. In statistics, that generally means thinking about and solving problems. And I don't mean just sitting down with a calculator and doing a lot of arithmetic. You need to think about what the problem calls for and how to go about structuring an answer. Only then should you add up the numbers and solve the equations. Don't be misled by the fact that much of the space in the Solutions section is devoted to arithmetic. That is just the nature of the task. How you go about solving a problem and how you interpret the answer may take less space to state, but they are certainly the more important part of the exercise.

I have included answers to only half of the exercises so that your instructor can assign problems for which you are on your own. But if you can do the problems that are covered here, you should be able to solve the other problems with little difficulty.

These solutions were worked and checked using a mixture of calculators and computer software. Answers often differ (sometimes by a surprising amount) depending on how many decimal places the calculator or program carries or how many intermediate steps you write down in truncated form. It is important not to be too concerned about small differences. These may be attributable to rounding (or the lack thereof) in intermediate steps. By looking at the intermediate steps, you can tell if you are solving the problem correctly. If you are, minor differences in the final result are not critical.

David Howell
University of Vermont
David.Howell@uvm.edu
June, 1994

Part I

Data Analyses Using StataQuest

INTRODUCTION

This short manual is intended to get you started doing data analysis with the StataQuest program. The emphasis is on using that program to derive useful and interesting results from data. I firmly believe that if you work along with me using your own copy of StataQuest, you will very quickly come to feel that you can work out any analysis on your own. (If you make a mistake, just try again. And if that doesn't work, press F1 (or ⌘1) and read the Help screens—they are very good.) I will certainly not cover all of the possible analyses, but I will cover enough that you will have sufficient background to go off on your own.

The first part of this discussion of StataQuest is concerned with the basics of running the program. You should read (and practice) all of this section the first time you sit down with StataQuest. Next is a demonstration of StataQuest's graphical and statistical procedures working through the analysis of several data sets. This latter discussion is organized along the lines of the text, and covers different analyses in roughly the same order I cover them in the book, although there are some minor differences. I suggest that you work through as much of the material as you feel comfortable with the first time, rather than wait on each section as you come to it in the text. You need the experience of running a set of analyses, even if you have not yet discussed those analyses in class. There may come a time when you will find yourself in over your head as far as the statistical aspects of the problem are concerned. If so you can stop and let the course catch up with you, or jump to the next section. I have tried to put the most general material first so that those who don't go all the way through the first time will at least have the basics. But the more you do, the more comfortable you will feel.

GETTING STARTED

Many software authors complain that users don't read manuals anymore; they just want to hop right in with both feet and get going. Rather than complain, I'll tell you how to get started and then lead you through the rest of the manual to show you how to perform typical analyses. Although StataQuest looks almost exactly the same whether you are running it from a PC (using DOS) or a Macintosh, there are differences in the way you install the program on your machine, how you start it up, and how you print out results and graphs. For that reason I will start with separate sections for DOS and Macintosh. Read the one that applies to you. Once you get beyond those two sections, the rest is the same.

DOS Machines

Before running StataQuest, you should install it on your PC. It will run faster that way, and you won't have to worry about doing something that damages the original copy of the program.

Installation

StataQuest can be run from the 3.5-inch floppy disk that is found in the back of the manual. However, most machines have a hard drive and I recommend installing it on your hard drive and running it from there. If for some reason you can't do that or don't wish to, then you can skip this section.

StataQuest is very easy to install. You just need to follow these few simple steps.

• Insert the StataQuest disk into a floppy disk drive and make that drive the current drive (for example, type "a:" and press ENTER).

• Type GO, and press ENTER.

• Select Install from the menu and follow the prompts.

• Now remove the floppy disk and store it safely away. You may need it to reload StataQuest in the future, and you certainly don't want to risk writing over the stuff that is there.

Starting

The DOS version of StataQuest starts when you type in the command GO and press the ENTER key. You then select the *Start StataQuest* command from the utility menu. When given the opportunity, start the menu system by typing *m* at the . prompt.

StataQuest's Menu System in DOS

When you enter StataQuest's menu system by typing *m* at the command prompt, you will see a clear workspace on the screen and a menu at the top. It looks like this:

Files Edit Graphs Summaries Statistics Calculator F1 = help

On the main menu, the **Files** submenu will be highlighted. Press the down arrow key or the ENTER key, and a pull-down menu of **Files** commands (**Open, Save, Import ASCII,** and so on) will appear. If you want to open an existing StataQuest data file or import an ASCII data file, you use the up or down arrow key to highlight the desired command and then press the ENTER key. The command will then be executed, sometimes taking the form of showing more menus or giving you prompts. Press the ESC key once or twice and the pull-down menu or menus will retreat, leaving the main menu as it was before.

Keyboard basics:

- Use the left and right arrow keys to select (highlight) items on the main menu or the spreadsheet menu.
- Use the down arrow key or press the ENTER key to pull down submenus from menus.
- Press the ENTER key to execute the selected (highlighted) StataQuest command.
- Press the ENTER key after typing any response to StataQuest prompts.
- Press the ESC key to move one level up in the StataQuest menus.
- Press the F1 function key to get help on a menu command or menu prompts.
- Press the F5 function key to toggle logging of output on or off after **Files/Session logging** has been chosen and a log file established. (Boldface commands such as this mean to go to the **Files** menu and select **Session logging**.)
- In StataQuest's spreadsheet, press the F10 function key to activate the spreadsheet menu.
- In StataQuest's spreadsheet, as an alternative to the F10 key, simultaneously press the ALT key and the first letter of a spreadsheet menu item (for example, ALT-F for **Files**) to access submenus directly.
- In StataQuest's spreadsheet, use the arrow keys and the HOME, END, PGDN, and PGUP keys to move from cell to cell around the spreadsheet.
- You can get help at any time and no matter where you are in

StataQuest's menu mode by pressing the F1 function key.

That's a lot to remember, but don't worry, you'll figure it out easily.

Quitting

To exit from StataQuest, select **Files/Quit to OS** from the menu. If there are data in memory, StataQuest will ask whether it should save these data. You should save the data if you have changed them in memory and want to save the changes for subsequent use.

Printing

To print your output, choose **Files/Session logging** to set up a log file. A log file will contain your commands and the output (though not the graphs) from each. Once you establish a log file you can turn the log file on and off with the F5 key. Turning the log file off means that output will not be copied to the log file. When you exit StataQuest, select *Print Log File* from the utility menu.

To print graphs, first create the graph. StataQuest prompts you after you have seen the graph, asking whether you wish to *Save the graph for printing*. If you choose to save the graph you will be asked to supply a file name of up to 8 characters in length. StataQuest will supply the .gph extension. To print the saved graph, exit from StataQuest and choose *Print graph* from the utility menu to print on any printer compatible with the HP Laserjet or the Epson FX standard. (The log file can also be edited with any standard word processing program.) If the cursor hangs after the printing is finished, press the ENTER key once or twice.

Macintosh Machines

Before running StataQuest, you should install it on your PC. It will run faster that way, and you won't have to worry about doing something that damages the original copy of the program.

Installation

Installing StataQuest on your hard drive is just a matter of dragging files to the disk.

- Insert the floppy disk in the disk drive.

- Double-click the disk's icon to open it.

- Drag the StataQuest folder icon to wherever you want it on your hard drive. (The StataQuest program is contained within the StataQuest folder. That is the way it *must* be, so don't rename either the application or the folder.)

- Remove the floppy disk by dragging it to the trash and then put it safely away.

Starting

To start StataQuest, double-click on the StataQuest icon. That, and a bit of patience at first, is all there is to it.

StataQuest's Menu System on the Macintosh

When you enter StataQuest's menu system by typing *m* at the command prompt, you will see a clear workspace on the screen and a menu at the top. It looks like this:

Files   Edit   Graphs   Summaries   Statistics   Calculator   F1 = help

Use the mouse to click on the menu item you want and drag down the menu. Release on the item you want to select. The command will then be executed, sometimes taking the form of showing more menus or giving you prompts. If StataQuest shows you more menu items, select the appropriate item with the mouse. If StataQuest prompts you with a question, type in the answer and press the RETURN key. You can back out of any situation with the ESC key.

If you select **Edit/Spreadsheet** from the main menu, an entirely new menu for the spreadsheet will appear in place of the main menu. (Boldface commands such as this one containing "/" mean to go to the **Edit** menu and select the **Spreadsheet** entry.)

Keyboard basics:

- Use the mouse to drag down each menu item. When you release the mouse, StataQuest will execute the chosen command.
- Press the RETURN key after typing any response to StataQuest prompts.
- Press the ESC key to end any command you do not wish to continue.
- For help, hold down the OPTION key and drag to the appropriate menu item. Release the mouse. Help on the menu item will appear.
- After you select from the menu, StataQuest will often ask you questions. These are called "input dialog." For help during an input dialog, press F1 or ⌘1.
- Press the F5 function key to toggle logging of output on or off after **Files/Session logging** has been chosen and a log file established.
- In StataQuest's spreadsheet, use the arrow keys and the HOME, END, PGDN, and PGUP keys, if you have them on your keyboard, to move from cell to cell around the spreadsheet.

Quitting

To exit from StataQuest, select **Files/Quit to OS**. If there are data in memory, you will be asked whether they should be saved. You should save the data if you have changed them since they were first loaded and if you want those changes saved for future use. It is usually a good idea to save the file anyway unless you have a specific reason for not doing so.

Printing

To print your output, choose **Files/Session logging** to set up a log file. You will be asked to give the file a name between 1 and 8 legitimate characters in length. StataQuest will supply the extension ".log" at the end of the name. A log file will contain your commands and the output (though not the graphs) from each. Once you establish a log file you can turn the log file on and off with the F5 key. Turning the log file off means that subsequent output will not be copied to the log file. When you exit StataQuest, you print the log by double-clicking on the log file in your StataQuest folder. From the **Files** menu select **Settings** and supply any information, such as the date, that you want to see printed on the output. Then select **File/Print** from the main menus. Follow regular printing procedures from that point. (The log file can also be edited with any standard word processing program.)

To print graphs, first create the graph. StataQuest prompts you after you have seen the graph, asking whether you wish to **Save the graph for printing**. If you choose to save the graph you will be asked to supply a file name of up to 8 characters in length. StataQuest will supply the .gph extension. To print the saved graph, exit from StataQuest and double-click on the graph icon in the StataQuest folder, and then choose **File/Print** from the main menu. Follow regular printing procedures from that point.

THE FILES MENU

The **Files** menu is the one that you will use to **Read** and **Save** data, to turn on **Session logging**, and to **Quit** from the menu system or from StataQuest itself.

Open

When you enter and then save data in StataQuest, you create a "data set" containing not only the numerical values, but also any labels and variable names that apply to these variables. This is the data set with which StataQuest works. The **Open** selection opens an already existing StataQuest data set and puts it in memory so you can process it. StataQuest will prompt you for the name of the file to open. If you press ENTER without specifying a file name, it will list the names of data files in the current folder or directory and then ask again for the name of the file you wish to open. After you type a file name and press ENTER, StataQuest will list the number of observations, variable names and numbers, and variable labels if they have been defined.

Save

This saves the data currently in memory as a StataQuest data set. Once saved, the file can be retrieved and used later with the **Open** command. If the data are new, StataQuest will prompt you for a file name. File names can be a maximum of 8 legal characters (a legal character is any letter or number). (Macintosh users are bound by this length restriction as well.) Type a name for the file and press ENTER. StataQuest will save the file under that name in the current folder or directory.

Import ASCII

This command allows StataQuest to read a data file created by a non-StataQuest program, such as a word processor or a database manager. ASCII stands for American Standard Code for Information Interchange, and ASCII files are plain character text files. (They are sometimes called Text files.) Many different software programs can read and write them, allowing you to transfer data from one program to another without having to type the data in all over again.

StataQuest will accept ASCII files that contain numbers or periods. It will not accept string (nonnumerical) variables such as names. (Periods, as opposed to decimal points, that occur within numbers are used to represent missing values.) Each number or period must be separated from the others (delimited) by at least one blank space or by a comma. Be prepared to supply StataQuest with names for each variable in the order in which they appear in the file.

Export ASCII

This command lets you write the data for the variables you select to an ASCII file so that it can be read by a non-StataQuest program. You will need to give the output file a name and type the names or numbers of the variables you want included. String variables can be included.

Session Logging

This command creates a "log" file to record your work and the output that appears on the screen in a text file, which you can later edit and print (except graphs, which are saved separately after each is drawn to the screen).

When you start a log file, you will need to give it a name. The name can be 1 to 8 characters, using any letters or numbers. Make the name distinctive so that you will remember it latter. While the file is open, you can use the F5 function key as a toggle to suspend logging of output you don't want to save (log off), or to reactivate logging of output you do want to save (log on). Each time you do this, StataQuest will notify you which state it is in.

The log file is saved automatically when you exit StataQuest. Log files are ASCII text files that can be read by most word processing programs. To print log files, see the separate instructions on printing.

Maintenance

The **Maintenance** submenu has three helpful "housekeeping" commands. The **Directory** command lists the names of all files contained in the current folder or directory. The **Display** command displays the contents of any text file in the current folder or directory. Use this command to read log files and to check on ASCII data files. The **Erase** command erases a file from the current folder or directory.

Quit to OS

This command quits StataQuest and takes you back to the operating system. You will be prompted to save any data still in memory before exiting, and, on a DOS machine, given the option to print log files and graphs.

Quit Menus

This command takes you out of the menu system and into command mode. Type *m* at any time to return to the menu system.

THE EDIT/SPREADSHEET MENU

StataQuest's spreadsheet is a visual workspace for data entry and management. It organizes and displays your data in a row and column format. The columns are variables and the rows are observations. Almost all your work with data will be done in the spreadsheet. You will use the spreadsheet to enter your data into StataQuest from the keyboard. You will use it to label, edit, and save your data. You will use it to sort, display, and manipulate your data in various ways. The spreadsheet has its own menu system for doing these things

To enter the spreadsheet from StataQuest's main menu, select **Edit/ Spreadsheet**. If you do not have a data set in memory, StataQuest will prompt you to open one from existing files or to create a new one.

The following is a display of a portion of the typical StataQuest spreadsheet. It shows the spreadsheet menu and a matrix of rows and columns with a data set currently in memory:

```
Files Add Drop  Replace  Sort  Label  F1 = Help  F10 = Menu
Cell: Density[4] = 44.19736
```

```
Enter new value:  > <
         State     Pop1990     LandArea      Density    Region
1.     Alabama     4040587        51705     78.14683     South
2.      Alaska      550043       591004     .9306925  NonSouth
3.     Arizona     3665228       114000     32.15112  NonSouth
4.    ARKANSAS     2350725        53187   [44.19736]     SOUTH
```

9

At the top of the spreadsheet is the menu. Just beneath it is the current value of the highlighted cell. In the example the current value of the Density[4] cell is 44.19736. This is the value for the fourth observation, Arkansas, on the variable Density. Highlighting of that cell is represented here by bold type in square brackets. The symbol > < represents the blinking cursor on the screen that marks where your text will be displayed when you type in a new value for the currently highlighted cell. To enter a new value into the spreadsheet you must type in the values and then press ENTER or an arrow key.

There are limits to how much data you can put in the spreadsheet. The maximum number of variables (columns) is 25. The maximum number of observations (rows) is 600. The maximum total number of spreadsheet cells (rows times columns) is 4,000.

The spreadsheet accepts data for both numeric and string variables (such as names and labels). Periods (.) denote missing data.

Activating and using the Spreadsheet Menu

The spreadsheet menu offers a choice of the **Files**, **Add**, **Drop**, **Replace**, **Sort**, and **Label** submenus. Each submenu has its own specialized tools for data management. You would use **Files**, for example, to open an existing data file and place it in the spreadsheet. To activate the spreadsheet menu, DOS users either press the F10 key and use the arrow keys to select the submenu desired, or *simultaneously* press the ALT key and the key corresponding to the 1st letter of the relevant entry. Macintosh users use the mouse.

Moving the Cursor to Highlight Cells

In the spreadsheet matrix of rows and columns, a rectangular cursor on the screen will identify the currently highlighted cell. Before you do anything in the spreadsheet, it is critical to know the location of the currently highlighted cell. That location identifies both the variable (column) and the observation (row) being worked on in the spreadsheet. *Any* cell highlighted in a column will select that column for commands that operate on *variables* (for example, the command to drop a Variable from the spreadsheet). *Any* cell highlighted in a row will select that row for commands that operate on Observations (for example, the command to drop an Observation from the spreadsheet).

To move the highlight cursor around in the spreadsheet, use the arrow keys. The HOME key will move you to row 1, column 1, and the END key will move you to the last observation in a column.

FILES

Use the spreadsheet **Files** submenu to create a new data set in the spreadsheet (**New**), open and use an existing StataQuest data set (**Open**), save new or changed data sets permanently on disk (**Save**), and quit the spreadsheet to StataQuest's main menu (**Quit Editor**). ESC will also quit the editor. When you quit the spreadsheet, the data in memory stays in memory.

New

When you select **New**, StataQuest will prompt you for the number of observations and number of variables you wish to place in the spreadsheet. If you indicate R observations and C variables, it will then display a matrix of R rows, C columns, and R x C cells. Each cell will initially contain a period denoting missing data. Variables will be assigned the generic names x1, x2, x3, and so on. (These can later be renamed if you wish in the **Replace** submenu.)

To enter new data from the keyboard for the currently highlighted cell, type the data and press ENTER or the right arrow key. What you typed will appear in the cell and replace what was there before. The cursor will now highlight another cell, either below the first one (if you pressed ENTER) or to its right (if you pressed the right arrow key). Continue entering data in this manner until you are done.

To correct a cell that is in error, highlight the cell containing the incorrect data. Type the correct value and then press ENTER or the right arrow key. The new value for that cell will be shown.

Open

This command opens an existing StataQuest data file and places it in the spreadsheet for you. You need to know the name of the file, but can see a list of all file names by pressing the ENTER key without entering a name.

Save

This command saves the data currently in memory as a StataQuest data file. You need to provide a name for the file. Valid names have any letter or number in them and are up to 8 characters in length. (These rules apply to the Macintosh version as well.) Once saved, the file can be retrieved and used later with the **Open** command.

If you have a lot of data to enter into the spreadsheet, you should save the first chunk of it early using the **Save** command. Continue to do this with later chunks until you are done. That way you won't lose all of your data if something goes wrong.

Quit Editor

This command takes you out of the spreadsheet and back to the main menu.

Add

Use the **Add** submenu to add a new variable (column) to the spreadsheet (**Variable**), add a new observation (row) anywhere in the spreadsheet (**Observation**), add a new observation at the end of the spreadsheet (**Obs at end of data**), and insert a new cell into a spreadsheet (**Cell**).

Add/Variable

There will be times when you want to add a new variable to an existing spreadsheet. For example, you might wish to add data from the keyboard for a new variable for the same observations. Or you might want to create a new variable from existing spreadsheet data using the **Replace/Formula** command. Or perhaps you would like to generate artificial data for a new variable using the **Replace/Random numbers** command.

Before you can do these things you must first add a new variable to the spreadsheet. When you add a new variable, StataQuest will prompt you for a variable name. It will insert a new column in the spreadsheet under that variable name just to the *left* of the column containing the currently highlighted cell. The cells in the column for the new variable will initially contain periods denoting missing data. Highlight a cell in that column and then either begin entering data from the keyboard or use the **Replace/ Formula** or **Replace/Random numbers** command as appropriate.

Add/Observation

Use this command to add data for a new observation to an existing spreadsheet. StataQuest will insert a new row in the spreadsheet just *above* the row containing the currently highlighted cell. (Use **Add/Obs at end of data** to add a new row at the bottom of the spreadsheet.) The cells in the newly created row will initially contain periods denoting missing numeric data. Highlight a cell in that row and begin entering data from the keyboard.

Add/Obs at End of Data

Use this command to add data for a new observation in a new row to be located just below the last row of an existing spreadsheet. (Use **Add/Observation** to insert a new row anywhere else in the spreadsheet.)

Add/Cell

These are the data to be entered: However, you entered this:

	x1	x2	x3
1.	33	54	12
2.	77	41	98
3.	42	66	15
4.	55	37	29

	x1	x2	x3
1.	33	54	12
2.	77	41	15
3.	42	66	29
4.	55	37	

Obviously, you goofed. You accidentally skipped the value 98 for cell x3[2] and kept on typing, with the result that all cell values in the column from that point on are located one row higher than they should be. You could correct each wrong cell in that column, one by one, to make things right, but that can be a painful process if there are a lot of data to be changed. A better way is to use the **Add/Cell** command to correct alignment mistakes of this sort. In the example, highlight the x3[2] cell and use **Add/Cell** to change that cell to missing and push the values 15 and 29 down one row where they belong. All cells above the error will be unaffected. Now simply enter 98 in x3[2].

Drop

Use the **Drop** submenu to drop a variable from the spreadsheet (**Variable**), drop an observation from the spreadsheet (**Observation**), drop all observations from the spreadsheet that have a specified value on a given variable (**Observations**), or drop a cell from a spreadsheet column (**Cell**). *Warning*: If you **Drop** something and then **Save**, whatever you dropped is lost forever unless you made a duplicate copy of your data as a backup.

Drop/Variable

This command drops the variable that is located in the column of the highlighted cell. All variables in the spreadsheet to the right of the dropped variable will shift one column to the left.

Drop/Observation

This command drops the observation that is located in the row of the highlighted cell. All observations below it in the spreadsheet will move up one row. (Remember that an "observation" is a whole row of data, not just the contents of one cell.)

Drop/Observations

This drops all observations from the spreadsheet that have a specified value on a given variable. For example, you might wish to drop *all* observations (rows) from the spreadsheet in which the variable is Sex = *Male*. The column location of the highlighted cell selects that variable as the one that will determine which observations are to be dropped, so position the cursor over any cell in the Sex column that contains the code for *Male*. If you now execute the **Drop/Observations** command, all the data for all variables for rows where *Male* appears will disappear from the spreadsheet. You might then use the **File/Save As** command to save this file as *Female.dta*. (The **Save As** command allows you to supply a new name for the file, whereas the **Save** command saves the data to the currently active file.)

The **Drop/Observations** command is helpful if you want to perform analyses on subsets of data. For example, if you wanted to look at the correlation between two variables only using female subjects, you could drop the male subjects and then perform the analysis.

Warning: If you drop observations to analyze or save a subset of the data, and if you don't want to lose permanently the data you have dropped, then do not Save the modified spreadsheet data under its existing file name.

Drop/Cell

Imagine that these are the data to be entered in a spreadsheet::

	x1	x2	x3
1.	33	54	12
2.	77	41	98
3.	42	66	15
4.	55	37	29

You entered the data and the resulting spreadsheet looks like:

	x1	x2	x3
1.	33	54	12
2.	77	41	**12**
3.	42	66	98
4.	55	37	29

Notice what happened in the column for variable x3. In cell x3[2] you accidentally repeated the value 12 entered previously in cell x3[1] yet kept on typing, with the result that all cell values in the column from that point on are located one row lower than they should be. You could correct each wrong cell value in the column one by one, but it is easier to use **Drop/Cell** to correct alignment mistakes of this sort. It will simply drop the offending entry and move the remaining entries in that cell up one row.

Replace

Use the **Replace** submenu to generate random data for observations from a selected probability density function (**Random numbers**), enter formulae that transform existing variables or generate values for new ones (**Formula**), convert a string variable (one containing nonnumerical data) to a labeled numeric variable (**String to labeled**), convert a labeled numeric variable to a string variable (**Labeled to string**), and rename variables (**Rename variable**).

Replace/Random numbers

This command will replace the current cell values of a variable with random numbers generated by a theoretical probability density function. You may choose from the normal, binomial, chi-square, exponential, F, Student's t, uniform, and Poisson distributions and Integers. The latter will generate random integers between 0 and whatever upper limit you designate.

Example: You want to create an artificial data set consisting of 200 observations containing random data drawn from a normally distributed population having a mean of 100 and a standard deviation of 15. Use **Files/New** to create a spreadsheet data set with 200 observations and one variable. Highlight any cell in the x1 column, Use **Replace/Random**

numbers, and then select **Normal**. When prompted for the mean of the normal distribution, enter 100. When prompted for its standard deviation (SD), enter 15. The 200 cells in the x1 column will fill up with data randomly generated by that particular normal distribution.

Replace/Formula

This command will replace the current cell values of a selected variable with new values computed by a formula specified by you. Typically, you will **Add** a variable to the spreadsheet, give it a name, and then use the **Replace/Formula** command to write a formula to compute new values for the added variable.

Example: In your spreadsheet you have data for countries' total population (TotalPop) and land area in square miles (LandArea). You want to compute values for all countries on a new variable called Density, which you define as total population divided by land area. Use **Add/Variable** to add a new variable to the spreadsheet and name it Density. Highlight any cell in the new Density column. Select **Replace/Formula**. When prompted for the formula, type TotalPop/LandArea. (The cells in the selected column will fill up with computed values for Density for all observations.

Note: Formulae are equations. In specifying a formula, however, you enter only the right-hand side of the equation. Since the Density column was selected, StataQuest assumed that Density was to go on the left-hand side of the equation.

Arithmetic Operators in Formulae

StataQuest will accept the following arithmetic operators in formula expressions: + (additions), − (subtraction), * (multiplication), / (division), ^ (raise to a power), and the prefix − (negation).

Examples: TotalPop/LandArea, x1 + x2, (Q1 + Q2 + Q3)/3, x3^2, (x1 - 100)^2, 100*(x1/x2).

Functions in Formulae

The following functions may be used in formula expressions. Substitute an actual variable name for x, n, or s in each expression.

abs(x)	absolute value
atan(x)	arc-tangent returning radians

cos(x)	cosine of radians
exp(x)	exponent (i.e., e^x)
log(x)	natural logarithm
sin(x)	sine of radians
sqrt(x)	square root
real(s)	converts strings into numeric values
string(n)	converts real values to strings

Examples: 2*sqrt(x3) + 3*sqrt(x4), log(gnp), log(gnp)/log(10), exp(.066*20), real(income). Real(income) might be used if the numeric data for the variable income were accidentally stored as a string variable.

Replace/String to Labeled

This command will convert values for a selected string variable to labeled numeric values.

Example: You enter the values male and female into cells for the variable gender. These are not numeric values, so StataQuest classifies gender as a string variable. Later you try to use gender in a cross-tabulation. StataQuest refuses because a procedure like that can be carried out only on numbers and not on words like male and female. What do you do? First supply labels for the Gender variable (see below). Then highlight a cell in the column for the variable gender. Use the **Replace/String to labeled** command. For each observation, StataQuest will replace the string "female" with the number 1, and the string "male" with the number 2. These now become the underlying values for the variable gender. The words "female" and "male" will continue to be displayed in the spreadsheet cells as labels assigned to those values. Cross-tabulation and other procedures can now be performed on this numeric variable.

Replace/Labeled to String

This command will convert labeled numeric values for the selected variable to strings. To emphasize: This command will not work unless the numeric values are labeled. (See next page for a definition of "labeled.")

Example: The numeric variable gender in your spreadsheet has the value labels 1 = female and 2 = male. The labels female and male are displayed in the spreadsheet cells, but the underlying values are numeric (1 or 2). For some reason you want to convert the underlying numeric values themselves into the strings "female" and "male." Highlight a cell in the column for the variable gender. Use the **Replace/Labeled to string** command to replace

17

the numeric value 1 with the string "female" and the numeric value 2 with the string "male." The words "female" and "male" will continue to be displayed in the spreadsheet cells, only now as values (not merely as labels) for the string variable gender. Cross-tabulation and other procedures cannot be performed on this string variable.

Replace/Rename Variable

This command will rename a selected variable in the spreadsheet. One good use of this command is to replace the generic spreadsheet variable names (x1, x2, x3, and so on) with more informative names.

Example: The variable x2 in your spreadsheet is age. Highlight a cell in the x2 column. Use the **Replace/Rename variable** command to replace the name x2 with the name "age."

Legal variable names: A variable name may be any sequence of 1 to 8 characters (A to Z and a to z), digits (0 to 9), and underscores (_). The first character of a variable name must be either a letter or an underscore. Embedded blanks are not allowed.

StataQuest is case-sensitive. It will view the names abc, Abc, and ABC as representing three different variables. In addition, a few otherwise legal names (such as byte, double, log, float, with, in, and int) are reserved for StataQuest's internal use, and you will receive an error message if you use them.

Replace/Recode

This command will recode the values of a continuous variable, allowing you to do such things as code all subjects younger than 12 as 1, all subjects between 12 and 18 as 2, and all sujects 18 or over as 3. The program will prompt you for the necessary information, and will even display important descriptive statistics to help you decide where to set the break between categories.

Sort

Use this command to order spreadsheet observations from low to high (**Forwards**) or from high to low (**Backwards**) on the values of a specified variable.

Example: You want to order data for automobiles in your spreadsheet from low to high on the variable weight. Highlight a cell in the weight column. Use the **Sort/Forwards** command. The first row in the spreadsheet will now contain the lightest automobile; the last row contains the heaviest.

Label

Use the Label submenu to attach descriptive labels to variables (**Variable**), to the numeric values of a variable (**Values**), or to the data set itself(**Dataset**).

Variable Labels

Use **Label/Variable** to attach a descriptive label to a selected variable in the spreadsheet. The label may have a maximum of 31 characters. In the transit.dta data set, for example, the fedlsub variable has the label Federal Subsidy in $ Millions.

Value Labels

Value labels convey the meaning of a variable's numeric values or codes. Such labels are usually assigned only to categorical variables that have relatively few values. Value labels can be any strings up to a maximum of 8 characters, including embedded spaces.

Example: 1 = Female, 2 = Male for the variable gender.

Dataset Labels

A data set label briefly describes the contents of a data file. This label may be a maximum of 31 characters.

Example: UN Human Development Data, 1991.

USEFUL COMMAND MODE OPTIONS

StataQuest's spreadsheet menu commands will handle most of your data entry and data management needs. A number of additional data management tools are available only in command mode, and cannot be called up from menus. To move to the command mode select **Files/Quit menus**. To return to the menu mode, type *m*. Particularly useful are the order and recode commands.

Changing the Order of Variables (Columns) in the Spreadsheet

After performing a series of manipulations on a spreadsheet, the resulting order of columns may not be to your liking. The variable Z might be displayed in the first column, for example, followed by columns for Y, W, and X. You want the order to be W X Y Z. Use StataQuest's order command to set things right.

Example: . order W X Y Z

Recoding Variables

StataOuest's **Recode** command remaps the original values of a numeric variable to a new set of values according to specified rules. Original values unaffected by the rules remain unchanged. An important kind of recoding is now done by the **Replace/Recode** command, but complex recoding and the recoding of categorical variables is best done in the command mode.

Examples:

recode X 1=0 2=1	changes 1 to 0 and 2 to 1 in X
recode X 1 3 4 7=1 *=2	changes 1, 3, 4, and 7 to 1 and all other values to 2
recode X 9 = .	changes 9 to missing in X

Since information can be lost through recoding, you should make a copy of the variable to be recoded and then recode the copy. (The **Replace/Recode** menu does this automatically.) In the spreadsheet, to make an exact duplicate of the variable Group (let's call it NewGroup): (1) Use the **Add/Variable** command to create a new variable named NewGroup. (2) Highlight a cell in NewGroup. (3) Use the **Replace/Formula** command and type Group as the formula. Then leave the spreadsheet, enter command mode, and recode NewGroup.

At this point we have covered the basic material on using the menu system. The next three menu entries are **Graphs**, **Summaries**, and **Statistics**. These are the fundamental data analysis tools in StataQuest, and we will apply many of the procedures found there to one of several examples, starting with an example on air quality. The only menu item that I am not covering is the last one, named **Calculator**. Those that will be useful you can figure out on your own, and the others you can play with or ignore.

MEASURING THE QUALITY OF THE AIR WE BREATHE

What, you might wonder, does air quality have to do with statistics in the social sciences? Well, probably not a lot. But that doesn't make what follows a bad example; in fact it is a very good example. First, a little history.

In about November of 1993 someone submitted an electronic mail message asking for help with the analysis of data on two air quality monitoring instruments. They had put two instruments side by side for an extended period of time and collected data from both. Now they wanted to use those data to determine if the two instruments were giving the same result. In other words, were the machines comparable? Their specific question is not important, but it got me thinking. I needed to give an exam to my students in a few weeks, and it seemed that this example provided a wonderful exam question. There are a large number of things that you could (and should) do with the data to answer the general question, and this would give me a chance to see how creative my students were. I knew that some would object that they were students in psychology, and not in environmental engineering, and that such a test was blatantly unfair. So I pointed out that if these two instruments were instead two psychological scales used to measure people's responses to threatening situations, the situation would be completely familiar and they would be answering a psychological question. The same goes for you. If you prefer to think of these as measures of responses to threat, feel free. Frankly, after having written two books filled with examples from psychology, it is a relief to think about environmental engineering—about which I know next to nothing.

The data set named AirQual.dta is a StataQuest file that I created to represent a set of measurements from two instruments (InstA and InstB). These instruments sat side by side for 50 days measuring the same air, and we want to know whether there are any important differences between the two sets of measures. If not, then we can use the less expensive monitor and discard the more expensive one. If there are differences, then we know that we are going to have to do more work.

I created the data to illustrate a number of interesting points. (I wanted us to have something to talk about.) By the time we get through analyzing these data we should have learned something about data analysis and about the ways we can approach problems of comparability. We might also learn something about measurement.

THE DISTRIBUTION OF INDIVIDUAL VARIABLES

We will first read the data into StataQuest using **File/Open** and specifying the file name as AirQuality.dta. Then we will look at the distribution of each of the two sets of scores. If the instruments have been measuring the same air, their measurements should look pretty much alike. If they look different, that is one indication that something is amiss.

We will start by creating a histogram for each variable. To create the histogram I will choose Histogram from the Graph menu (denoted **Graph/ histogram**), request 10 intervals, and ask to have a normal distribution superimposed. I decided on 10 intervals because I peeked at the results of 8 intervals and wished that I had more. I am asking for the normal distribution simply because it gives us a frame of reference for looking at the resulting histogram. The results are shown below.

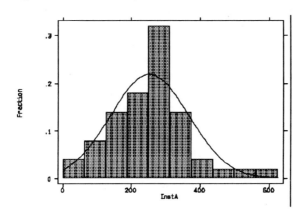

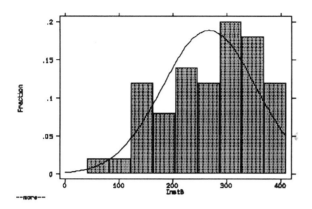

--more--

Notice that the first distribution is positively skewed with a center somewhere around 250. The second distribution (InstB) has a different shape. It is negatively skewed, but my eye is not good enough to estimate the center of the distribution. The difference in shape isn't terribly good news for the people who made the instruments, because they would want similar readings and hence similar shapes. Notice that Instrument A produced a few readings in the 500–600 range, whereas Instrument B never produced anything over about 400. That's an important clue to which we will return.

Histograms are not the only way to plot data; nor are they necessarily the best way. We could look at stem-and-leaf displays, but I will leave that to you as an exercise. Just select **Graphs/Stem and Leaf**.

One interesting plot worth seeing is the boxplot. Boxplots illustrate skewness nicely, and can be aligned to make comparisons easier. StataQuest produces very useful boxplots by not only plotting the boxplot for each variable, but also by superimposing, on the axis, tick marks representing each data point. This gives you a sense of how the actual data are spread out along the scale. To draw these boxplots, select **Graph/Comparison of variables/Boxplot + one-way**. In response to the first query, list the two variables we want to plot (InstA InstB). When it asks if you want to scale each variable, answer "no." This will mean that both variables will be plotted on the same scale for purposes of comparison. The resulting plot is shown below.

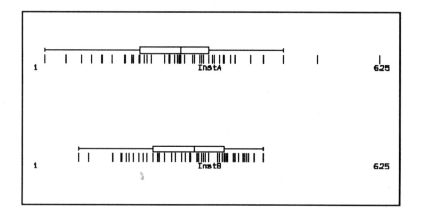

Here you can see clearly the difference between the two distributions. By looking at the tick marks (vertical lines), we can identify individual data points. Instrument A has a few readings somewhat lower than the lowest readings of Instrument B, and several readings that are considerably higher than the highest readings on Instrument B. The skewness is there, but it is not as noticeable as it was in the histograms.

As you can tell from the **Graph** menu, there are many other graphs that we could have calculated. I will leave exploration of these options to you; the procedures are quite straightforward.

DESCRIPTIVE STATISTICS

Having looked at the shape of the distributions, let's calculate some simple descriptive statistics. Those of you who like to play with programs without bothering to read the manual will no doubt discover a menu entry named **Summaries/Describe Data**. Well, forget it. That entry doesn't tell you anything you are likely to care about. It certainly won't give you descriptive statistics. Your next guess would probably be **Summarize/Means and SDs**, and that would certainly work. However, if you go farther down the menu to **Summarize/Data detail [medians...]** you will find something more to your liking. The results of that choice appear below for the two variables.

```
                              InstA
------------------------------------------------------------------
         Percentiles      Smallest
   1%           1               1
   5%          70              42
  10%         108.5            70        Obs                 50
  25%         180              89        Sum of Wgt.         50

  50%         257                        Mean             252.66
                           Largest       Std. Dev.        113.9478
  75%         309             410
  90%         372.5           447        Variance        12984.11
  95%         447             510        Skewness          .5380016
  99%         625             625        Kurtosis         4.411977

Press any key to continue
```

```
                              InstB
------------------------------------------------------------------
         Percentiles      Smallest
   1%          65              65
   5%         130              84
  10%         146             130        Obs                 50
  25%         205             144        Sum of Wgt.         50

  50%         282                        Mean             266.98
                           Largest       Std. Dev.        86.57154
  75%         338             380
  90%         375.5           384        Variance        7494.632
  95%         384             394        Skewness         -.3957006
  99%         410             410        Kurtosis         2.256637

Press any key to continue
```

Here you see most of the descriptive statistics you are likely to want, and some you don't care about at all. Notice that the two instruments differ by 25 points in the median and by about 14 points in the mean for the same air samples. Notice also that the standard deviation for Instrument A is noticeably larger than the standard deviation for Instrument B, possibly owing to the two or three extreme scores in Instrument A's data.

NORMAL DISTRIBUTIONS AND OTHER INTERESTING THINGS

I am trying to track along more or less with the text, and now we come to material covered in Chapter 6 on the normal distribution. This presents a problem because the two distributions we have seen so far are not very normally distributed, and it is hard to say anything substantive about them in this section. I can get around this problem by generating a new data set that contains, among other things, a normally distributed variable. This data set is on the disk and is named Distrib.dta. I created the three variables in that data set by clicking on **Edit/Spreadsheet/New** and telling the program that I want 400 observations. I then used the arrow keys to place my cursor in the first column of the spreadsheet and clicked the mouse on **Replace/Random Numbers/Normal.** In answer to the query I said that I wanted a mean of 0 and a standard deviation of 1. After a pause, the spreadsheet returns with 400 observations drawn at random from a normally distributed population.

But I don't want to stop here. While I'm generating variables I should generate at least one variable that is not normal, so that we have a base of comparison. Here I'm going to generate a sample of 400 observations that follows what is called the F distribution on 1 and 10 degrees of freedom. (We will consider what that description means when we come to Chapter 16.) I can name the variables by putting the cursor in the column that I want to rename and choosing **Replace/Rename variable** from the menu.

This distribution of the normal variable is shown below. It was plotted by exiting the Spreadsheet menu (by pressing the **Esc** key) and choosing **Graph/One variable/Histogram**. I then answered Normal, 40, and yes to the queries.

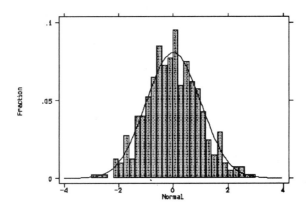

You can see that this distribution is reasonably close to a normal distribution. There are a few bumps and wiggles caused by the fact that we have a sample of 400 cases from a larger population, and in any sample chance will cause some observations to be slightly more frequent than they are expected to be, and others less frequent. However, the normal curve that has been superimposed does fit the distribution reasonably well.

26

Next, let's go to a distribution that is decidedly not normal. We can generate a sample from a population having an *F* distribution by going to the spreadsheet (**Edit/Spreadsheet**), moving our cursor to the second column, and entering **Replace/Random Numbers/F**, and responding with 1 and 10 when asked for the degrees of freedom for the numerator and denominator. This distribution is plotted using **Graph/One variable/Histogram** and responding F, 40, and yes to queries from StataQuest.

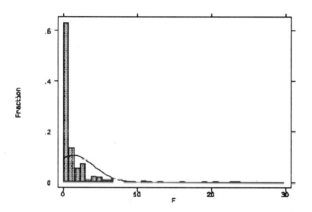

Notice how different is the shape of this distribution. First of all there are no values less than 0, which truncates the distribution on the left. Second, the distribution is very positively skewed, so the values on the right go much farther out than we would expect from a normal distribution. You can see the normal curve superimposed for comparison purposes.

I told you that I had drawn the normal data from a population where $\mu = 0.00$ and $\sigma^2 = 1.00$. From the table of z in the appendix we know that for a distribution with a mean of 0 and a standard deviation of 1.00, 75% of a normal distribution lies below $z = 0.67$, 90% lies below $z = 1.28$, 95% lies below $z = 1.64$, and 99% lies below 2.33. (Similar values apply to the other end of the distribution. We can make use of the descriptive statistics to see how that distribution compares to what we would expect.)

I can obtain the descriptive statistics by calling up **Summaries/Data detail** and entering Normal as the name of the variable. The results of that analysis are shown below.

```
.  summarize Normal,  detail

                               Normal
---   --------------------------------------------------------
       Percentiles      Smallest
 1%     -2.062259       -2.901898
 5%     -1.683657       -2.574161
10%      -1.3758        -2.179221      Obs                  400
25%      -.799191       -2.099257      Sum of Wgt.          400

50%      -.0594822                     Mean           -.0557979
                         Largest       Std. Dev.        1.00068
75%       .5777834       2.378206
90%      1.298935        2.458646      Variance        1.001361
95%      1.594885        2.463169      Skewness        .0999287
99%      2.363648        3.000878      Kurtosis        2.70906
```

Here we see that the mean of our sample is -0.056, with a standard deviation of almost exactly 1.00. These values are quite close to the population values, which is a satisfying state of affairs. Next we see that the 75th percentile is at 0.58, whereas we had expected it to be at 0.67. The 25th percentile, at the other end of the distribution, is at -0.80, which overshoots slightly in the opposite direction. For the 90th , 95th, and 99th percentiles we obtained 1.30, 1.59, and 2.36 where we had expected 1.28, 1.64, and 2.33, respectively. That is pretty good agreement. (Looking at the negative end of the distribution, we have −1.38, −1.68, and −2.06. We didn't do quite as well there, but it could be worse.)

The point of this last section was twofold. First I wanted to show you that when we actually draw a large sample from a normal population, the data come out about as predicted from the tables of the normal distribution. Second, I wanted to show you that everything is not perfect. Even with 400 cases, the values are off slightly. This is just random error, and is what we would expect. If you repeat what I did by drawing a new sample, you will also be off, but in different ways. In other words, your 75th percentile might be a little too high rather than a little too low.

THE CORRELATION OF AIR QUALITY MEASURES

Let's return to the air quality data that we were using before. (Again, if you would prefer to think of those data as two measures of response to threatening situations, that's fine too.) When we ask whether two instruments give comparable readings, one of the most obvious things to ask is "What is the correlation between those two measures?" Although correlations are not everything, we would certainly look askance at two instruments that claimed to be measuring the same thing, but whose measures were not highly correlated.

However, before we look at the correlation between our measures, it is prudent to plot those variables against one another. That plot will give us a sense of the linearity of the relationship, will point out unusual data points, if any, and will give us a different view of our data. The following scatterplot was generated in StataQuest by **Graph/Scatterplot/Y vs. X, with regression line**, specifying InstB as the Y variable and InstA as the X variable. I chose to fit a regression line because it helps to put the plot in perspective and because we will need that line shortly when we get to regression.

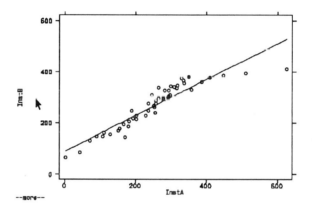

--more--

This plot tells us several interesting things. The most apparent thing that we see is that the best-fitting line is probably curvilinear. The points rise linearly up to about X = 400, and then flatten out noticeably. A second thing that we see, related to this curvilinearity, is that Instrument B seems to reach a plateau at about 400 units. It doesn't record much above 400 even when Instrument A has a reading of over 600.

A third thing to notice is that in the center of the scale the data points from Instrument B seem to be above those for Instrument A. Perhaps this is just a trick played on our eye by the presence of the regression line. I leave to you the task of fitting a new regression line to a data set excluding those cases where InstA is greater than 400. (The **Drop/Observations** command won't help here because it wants to drop observations with specific values. We want to drop those with a range of values. Instead, use the **Files/Quit menus** command to leave the menu system. Then at the "." prompt, enter

29

keep if InstA < 400. Now restart the menu system by typing **m** and replot the data. What do you find? If you wish you may use **File/Save** to save the file under the name Temp, but there is probably no reason to save this data set. To get back to the original data file, chose **Files/Open** and specify AirQual.dta again.)

We have learned at least two important things about Instrument B so far. We saw that it was negatively skewed, and we saw that it seems to have a built-in ceiling, so that it won't give readings much above 400. That is like driving a car whose speedometer won't register over 50. Driving around town, it doesn't matter. But the minute you get on the Interstate, you have a problem. These two things that we have learned are not independent. One reason why the distribution is negatively skewed is because extreme values do occur on InstA, but are not allowed to occur on the InstB.

Now let's go a bit farther and examine the correlation coefficient itself. We can calculate the correlation from **Statistics/Correlation/Regular [Pearson]**. When the program asks for the variable names, write them out sequentially, with a space between, without pressing the RETURN key until you are done. In this case, just enter "InstB InstA." The matrix that results is shown below, where we can see that the correlation between the two variables is very high ($r = .9268$).

```
. correlate  InstB InstA
(obs=50)

           |    InstB       InstA
-----------+------------------------
     InstB |   1.0000
     InstA |   0.9268     1.0000
```

In most situations we would be delighted to have a correlation of nearly .93. However, when our two variables are supposedly physical measures of the same thing, a correlation of .93 doesn't look quite so good. But, the more serious problem from the point of view of comparing the two instruments is the ceiling effect, and resulting curvilinearity, that we saw above.

30

WHAT CAN REGRESSION TELL US?

There is even more to learn, however, if we run a standard regression analysis on these data. We can compute the regression by specifying **Statistics/Simple regression**. We then select InstB as the Y variable and InstA as the X variable. The results follow.

```
. regress InstB InstA

  Source |      SS        df        MS                Number of obs =      50
---------+------------------------------             F( 1,   48) =  292.27
   Model | 315432.547      1   315432.547            Prob > F      =  0.0000
Residual | 51804.4331     48   1079.25902            R-square      =  0.8589
---------+------------------------------             Adj R-square  =  0.8560
   Total | 367236.98      49   7494.63224            Root MSE      =  32.852


   InstB |    Coef.   Std. Err.        t     P>|t|      [95% Conf. Interval]
---------+--------------------------------------------------------------------
   InstA |  .704124    .0411869     17.096    0.000      .6213123    .7869358
   _cons | 89.07602    11.3963       7.816    0.000     66.16222    111.9898

Press any key to continue
```

In the upper left, we see the Analysis of Variance table testing the null hypothesis that there is no relationship between the variables. The *F* for this test is 292.27, which is tucked away over on the right. The probability value for this *F* is given as 0.0000, meaning that the result is extremely unlikely to occur by chance if there were actually no relationship. This is not a terribly useful statistic, however, because there was no question about the *significance* of the relationship, only whether it is very high.

In the lower part of the table are the regression coefficients and tests on them. We are told that the optimal regression equation is

$$\hat{Y} = 0.704 \text{InstA} + 89.076.$$

We are then given the opportunity to plot this model, with or without showing confidence limits, and we can save the values of $\hat{Y}$ as a separate variable.

Both the slope and the intercept were significant by a t test at $p \leq 0.000$. Each of these coefficients tells us something, and we'll start with the intercept. You will recall that the intercept is the value of Y (InstB) when X (InstA) = 0. The results tell us that even when InstA records no pollution in the air, we expect InstB to report 89 units. Not very encouraging! If one instrument says there is no pollution, so should the other. Next, look at the slope. From our analysis we see that $b = 0.704$. For a one unit difference in InstA, we will only see a 0.704 unit difference in InstB. That means that when pollution levels rise and InstA increases by 10 units, for example, InstB will have shown only a 7.04-point rise. Again, that is not very reassuring. It certainly looks as if we have an instrument that needs adjustment. Compared to Instrument A, Instrument B reads too high for low levels of pollution, is less sensitive to differences in pollution levels, and peaks out at about 400 units. While it is possible that Instrument B is just fine, and that it is Instrument A that is wrong, the ceiling effect we see suggests that B is at fault.

TESTING MEANS WITH t

There is one more question we can ask of these data. The original query on electronic mail had asked how to tell whether there was a significant difference between the means. As you probably can guess, the correct answer here is a t test. The writer's actual question was whether it should be a paired-sample t or an independent-sample t. As we have already seen, there is a very high correlation between the two variables. There is no way that we can consider the two sets of measures as independent, and so a paired-sample t is our only possibility.

To perform a t test for two related samples, select the command **Statistics/Parametric tests/2-sample t tests**. You will be given a choice of three possible tests, and you should choose the last one and respond with "3." When asked for "Variable to be tested," don't panic. It really means *first* variable to be tested. Answer InstA. To the query "Second variable to be tested," answer InstB. When asked for the "confidence level in percent," press ENTER unless you want something other than a 95% interval. The resulting output follows.

```
. ttest InstA =InstB,   level(95)

 Variable |         Obs          Mean    Std. Dev.
----------+----------------------------------------
    InstA |          50        252.66    113.9478
    InstB |          50        266.98    86.57154
----------+----------------------------------------
    diff. |          50        -14.32    46.83904

            Ho:  diff = 0  (paired data)
                        t = -2.16 with 49 d.f.
             Pr > |t| = 0.0355
    95% conf. interval = (-27.6315, -1.0085)
Press any key to continue
```

Notice that, as we saw earlier, InstA has a mean that is about 14 points below the mean of InstB, but with a standard deviation that is somewhat higher (probably due to the ceiling effect on InstB). The t on H_0: μ_A - μ_B = 0 is -2.16 with 49 df. The probability of a t this extreme (i.e., a two-tailed test) is .0355. Since .0355 is less than .05, we will reject H_0 and conclude that Instrument B does read significantly higher, on average, than Instrument A. (This is a good place for you to try out the menu item **Calculator**. Choose **Calculator/Statistical tables/Student's t** and enter 49 and -2.16. What do you find? The small difference between the probabilities for t given by the t test and by the calculator is probably due to the fact that the printout rounds t to two decimal places, but the program calculates the probability using many more.) Our t test answers the question about whether the two population's means are different, but in light of what we already know about the slope of the regression line, the question may be meaningless. Since the slope is less than 1, for low values from Instrument A we expect Instrument B to read at least relatively higher, and for high values for Instrument A we expect Instrument B to read relatively lower. How the means themselves behave may simply be missing the point. Also notice how wide our 95% confidence interval is.

RUNNING t TESTS FOR INDEPENDENT SAMPLES

I don't want to pass by t tests without discussing how you would conduct a t test to compare the means of two independent samples, but it would not make sense to demonstrate that test with respect to the data we have been using, because these are paired data. For this purpose I will use a different data set on religious fundamentalism that is also found on the disk.

First we need to load the data file for our example. This file is located in the StataQuest directory or folder and is named Optimism.dta. Select **File/ Open**. If you already have a file open, it will ask if you want to save it. If you want to save it, type "yes" to each question; otherwise type "no." When asked for the name of the file to open, enter "Optimism.dta." To see what the variables look like, press **Summaries/Means and SDs**, and press "ENTER" when asked for the names of variables. Since the means are averaged across groups, they only give us a general idea what the data look like. The first five variables have 250 cases, while the sixth has only 170. These variables will be explained in the next section.

THE GLOOMY LIBERAL

Have you ever noticed that liberals often think that the world is a pretty gloomy place? And it isn't just people who are politically liberal who act that way—religious liberals are like that too. On the other hand, it has been suggested that those with a more fundamentalist religious faith have a relatively sanguine view of the world, perhaps because they see life in a broader context. Indeed, Marx is quoted as saying that "Religion is the opiate of the people," although whether Marx had any unique insight into this problem is perhaps questionable. Certainly those with more liberal views of religion take to themselves a greater responsibility for the conduct of their own lives, whereas the more fundamentalist sects or religions encourage their followers to accept a hierarchical structure in which faith in authority is expected of all. An unquestioning faith might be expected to lead to less concern with the cares of the world, which in turn might lead to a greater optimism about the world and one's place in it. At least that's a theory.

Sethi and Seligman (1993) reported a study in which they looked at the relationship between optimism and religious fundamentalism. They were concerned with two broad issues. The first was whether the three different groups varied in their level of optimism. The second was whether optimism could be predicted on the basis of several different variables related to the role of religion in the person's life.

Sethi and Seligman collected data from over 600 adults from nine religious groups. They sorted these nine groups into three major categories: (1) Fundamentalists, (2) Moderates, and (3) Liberals, and used those three categories for their analyses. They then collected data on Optimism and three variables that measure the role of religion in the person's life.

The Optimism measure that Sethi and Seligman collected was calculated from the Attributional Style Questionnaire, on which a score of 0.0 represents a neutral position between optimism and pessimism, a negative score represents pessimism, and a positive score represents optimism.

Sethi and Seligman also used a questionnaire designed to measure religiosity. They assessed the influence of religion in daily life (Influen) using questions such as, "To what extend do your religious views influence who you associate with?" They measured religious involvement (Involve) with questions such as, "How often do you attend religious services?" Finally, they measured religious hope (Hope) with questions such as, "Do you believe there is a heaven?" Each of these items was rated on a 7 point Likert scale (where 7 = strongly agree), and the individual's mean across the items on each scale was used as the dependent variable.

BACK TO THE ANALYSES

Now we are ready to run our *t* test. The data are contained in a file named Optimism.dta. The major reason for collecting these data in the first place was to compare religious liberals and fundamentalists on the Optimism variable. I created a variable named "Fund_Lib which is coded "1" for those respondents who are classed as Fundamentalists, "3" for those who are classed as Liberal, and missing (denoted as a ".") for the Moderates. The Moderates will be dropped from this test as missing.

To compute the *t* test, select **Statistics/Parametric tests/2-sample t** and respond "1" to the next query. We responded with a "1" here because our dependent variable (Optimism) is in one column and our independent (grouping) variable is in column Fund_Lib." (If we had placed the Fundamentalists' scores in one column and the Liberals' scores in another, we would have responded "2.") The program will then ask for the variables to be tested, and you respond "Optim." When asked for the variable defining the groups, respond "Fund_Lib." Finally, when asked if you wish to pool the variances, answer "yes." Again, press ENTER if you wish for 95% confidence intervals on the difference between population means. The results of the *t* test follow.

```
.  ttest Optim,   by(FundLib) level(95)

   Variable |        Obs          Mean      Std. Dev.
   ---------+---------------------------------------
        1 |        120      3.066667       2.935535
        3 |         50           .44       3.078298
   ---------+---------------------------------------
   combined |        170      2.294118       3.202527

           Ho:   mean(x) - mean(y) = 0  (assuming equal variances)
                                   t = 5.24 with  168 d.f.
                          Pr > |t| = 0.0000
                95% conf. interval = (1.6371, 3.6162)
Press any key to continue
```

You can see that the means are quite far apart. The Liberals have a mean of 0.44, which is only slightly on the optimistic side of neutral, while the Fundamentalists have a mean of 3.07. Notice that the standard deviation for both groups is about 3, which tells us that the difference between the means is almost a full standard deviation.

The *t* test is given below the table of means, and $t = 5.24$, which, on 168 *df*, is significant with a probability level beyond 0.0000. Clearly, religious fundamentalists have a significantly (and substantially) more optimistic view of the world that religious liberals. Notice that the 95% confidence interval is well away from 0.00.

We chose to pool the variance, and with standard deviations that close, it certainly looks as if that was the correct decision. If you are unsure, you can use the **Statistics** menu to select a test on the equality of variances, and that test will confirm that there is no significant difference. Interestingly, if you had gone ahead and not pooled, you would have obtained the same *t*, but the degrees of freedom would have been substantially less—though not so much less as to endanger the significance of the result. Why don't you try running that test for practice?

THE ANALYSIS OF VARIANCE: COMPARING THREE RELIGIOUS GROUPS

The *t* test only allows us to compare two groups, whereas a one-way analysis of variance will allow us to compare all three groups simultaneously. Since I would like to see how all three groups compare, the analysis of variance is the obvious choice, with Optim as the dependent variable and Group as the independent, or grouping, variable. The normal way to run the analysis of variance is to select **Statistics/ANOVA/One-way** from the menus. When asked for the dependent variable enter "Optim," and when asked for the independent variable enter "Group." The one problem with this approach is that the menu system does not allow us to specify comparisons between groups, which is something that I would like to see. I suggest that you issue the commands described above, to make sure you understand how to run the standard analysis, and then continue.

If we leave the menu system we can issue a more complete command that will produce the Scheffé and Bonferroni tests of group differences. To issue commands without the menu, first notice what commands Stataquest generates when you select from menus. For the one-way this was "one-way Optim Group." Now get out of the menu structure by entering **Files/Quit menus**. This will leave us with just a period as a prompt. If you enter the same StataQuest command that the program entered for itself (i.e., one-way Optim Group) you will repeat the same analysis of variance. However, if you instead enter "one-way Optim Group, scheffe" you will also produce Scheffé tests of group differences. Notice the capitalization, or lack thereof, and notice the comma that separates the main command from the subcommand. The results of this analysis follow on the next page, where I have included the command that produced it. (Can you guess how you would run Bonferroni tests?)

The first part of this table looks like others we have seen. It gives the means and standard deviations of each of the three groups, and then follows this with the analysis of variance summary table. That table contains the Between and Within groups *SS* and *MS*, and computes an *F*. This $F = 13.52$, which the next column tells us is significant at a probability value of 0.0000 (to 4 decimal places). We can conclude that the three religious groups differ in their level of Optimism. However, we cannot tell from this result which group(s) are more optimistic.

Bartlett's test follows the analysis of variance summary table. It is a test on the equality of population variances. Without knowing anything further about the test, you can see that the probability value associated with this test is 0.690, which is not remotely close to significant. Since we are testing $H_0: \sigma^2_1 = \sigma^2_2$, failure to reject H_0 means that we have no reason to think that there are unequal population variances. Therefore, we can feel reasonably confident that the underlying assumption of homogeneity of variance is satisfied.

```
. oneway Optim Group,   tabulate

                |        Summary of Optim
          Group|     Mean    Std. Dev.          Freq.
        --------+-------------------------------------------
              1 |   3.0666667   2.9355352           120
              2 |         1.9   3.2044273            80
              3 |         .44    3.078298            50
        --------+-------------------------------------------
          Total |       2.168   3.2019974           250

                        Analysis of Variance
         Source            SS         df      MS              F      Prob > F
        -----------------------------------------------------------------------
        Between groups    251.957333    2   125.978667      13.52     0.0000
        Within groups    2300.98667   247   9.31573549
        -----------------------------------------------------------------------
          Total          2552.944    249   10.2527871

    Bartlett's test for equal variances:  chi2(2) =   0.7415  Prob>chi2 = 0.690


                        Comparison of Optim by Group
                                 (Scheffe)


     Row Mean - |
     Col Mean   |        1                2
     -----------+------------------------------------
            2   |    -1.16666
                |     0.032
                |
            3   |    -2.62667        -1.46
                |     0.000          0.031
```

The section in the table on Scheffé's test may not be completely obvious. Notice the entry in the upper left, −1.16666, is the difference in means between group 2 (Moderates) and group 1 (Fundamentalists). The difference is negative, meaning that the Fundamentalists have a higher optimism score that the Moderates. Scheffé's test on this difference is significant at the .032 level, which, because it is less than .05, causes us to reject the null hypothesis of equality. In the bottom row we see that the difference between Liberals and Fundamentalists is −2.62667, with an associated p value of .000. (This is the same difference we tested above with a t test.) Finally, the difference between the Liberals and the Moderates is

−1.46, which is significant at the $p = .031$ level. From these results we can conclude that the groups are ordered on Optimism from the Fundamentalists at the more optimistic end, through the Moderates, and finally to the Liberals at the least optimistic end. These differences have all been shown to be significant. Relatively speaking, we liberals are a pretty gloomy group.

ACCOUNTING FOR OPTIMISM: MULTIPLE REGRESSION

I have broken the sequence in the book somewhat by postponing a discussion of multiple regression until I had something meaningful to say. Now that we have shown that religious groups differ in their degree of optimism, it makes sense to see if we can look at optimism from a slightly different direction. When Sethi and Seligman (1994) collected their data on Optimism, they also collected data on religious involvement, the influence of religion on people's daily lives, and people's religious hopes for the future. I'm curious to see how these four variables (Optim, Influen, Involve, and Hope) fit together, and to see if the religious variables can account for a large proportion of the variability in people's optimism.

We will first examine the correlations among these four variables by selecting **Statistics/Correlation/Regular (Pearson)** from the menu, and then specifying the variables. Since you have made it this far, I assume that you don't need instruction on how to do that. The results are shown below.

```
. correlate  Optim Influen Involve Hope
(obs=250)

         |     Optim    Influen    Involve       Hope
---------+-------------------------------------------
   Optim|    1.0000
 Influen|    0.2945     1.0000
 Involve|    0.2399     0.4757     1.0000
    Hope|    0.3035     0.4992     0.6080     1.0000
```

The first column gives the correlation of Optimism with each of the religious variables, and the other entries show how those variables are correlated among themselves. The correlations with Optimism are all about equal, ranging from .25 to .30. The intercorrelations of the religious variables are higher, ranging from .48 to .61.

For the multiple regression I have chosen to use all three religious variables as predictors. I obtained the following results by selecting **Statistics/Multiple regression** and entering the appropriate variable names. Note that here and in the preceding analysis, when asked for several variables together, you write them on the same line with a space between. (You can save typing and space by using the number of the variable instead of its name; i.e., instead of entering "Influen Involve Hope," you can enter "2 3 4.")

The results of this analysis follow.

```
. regress Optim  Influen Involve Hope

  Source |      SS        df       MS                    Number of obs =     250
---------+------------------------------                 F( 3,    246) =   11.21
   Model | 306.921185      3  102.307062                 Prob > F      =  0.0000
Residual | 2246.02282    246  9.13017405                 R-square      =  0.1202
---------+------------------------------                 Adj R-square  =  0.1095
   Total |  2552.944     249  10.2527871                 Root MSE      =  3.0216


----------------------------------------------------------------------------------
   Optim |    Coef.   Std. Err.       t      P>|t|      [95% Conf. Interval]
---------+------------------------------------------------------------------------
 Influen |  .4592891   .1802181     2.549    0.011      .1043217     .8142564
 Involve |  .0974386   .1981382     0.492    0.623     -.2928252     .4877024
    Hope |  .4161068   .1733521     2.400    0.017       .074663     .7575505
   _cons | -2.431301   .8211081    -2.961    0.003     -4.048599    -.8140016
----------------------------------------------------------------------------------

Press any key to continue
```

This table is very much like the one you saw earlier with respect to simple regression, so I won't repeat what I said there. I will simply note that the overall regression is significant ($F = 11.21$, $p = 0.0000$), meaning that there is better than a chance relationship between Optimism and the religious variables taken together.

The bottom half of the table gives us the slopes and the intercept. From these entries I can write

$$\hat{Y} = 0.459*Influen + 0.097*Involve + 0.416*Hope - 2.431.$$

The t values in the fourth column represent tests on the significance of each regression coefficient (slope or intercept). We see that the t's for Influen, Hope and the Intercept (denoted _cons) are all significant, meaning that these coefficients are reliably different from 0. As Influen increases by 1 point, our predicted level of Optimism increases by 0.459, *assuming that all other predictors are held constant.* Similarly, for people who differ by one point on Hope, we would expect their Optimism scores to differ by 0.416 points.

The *t* value for Involve was not significant, meaning that we have no reason to conclude that there is a relationship between Optimism and religious Involvement once we take the other variables into account. This might suggest to you that it would be worthwhile to repeat this analysis with Involve omitted. I leave that exercise to you.

In the lower right of the table you see the 95% confidence intervals. The first one can be interpreted to mean that the probability is .95 that the interval 0.104–0.814 contains the true value of the parameter. (As I said in the text, this is strictly not correct, and some people start pounding the table and stamping their feet when they see it written that way. Technically all we can say is that an interval formed in the way we formed this one has a 95% probability of bracketing the parameter it is trying to estimate. If that sounds like "nitpicking," perhaps it is.)

From the results of our regression solution we see that Optimism is positively related to the influence of religion on people's lives and their religiously based hopes for the future. When those variables are controlled, religious involvement does not make a significant contribution.

DISTRIBUTION-FREE METHODS WHEN POPULATIONS ARE NOT NORMAL

If you think back to where this all started, we began with two instruments for measuring air quality. One of the odd things about those two measures was that not only were they skewed, but they were skewed in opposite directions—not drastically, but somewhat. Because one of the assumptions behind the *t* test is that our samples were drawn from normally distributed variables (or at least symmetrically distributed ones), you might have some qualms about the *t* test we ran comparing the means of the two samples of observations. You might ask what would happen if we ran the distribution-free Wilcoxon signed-ranks matched-pairs test instead. That test relaxes the assumptions about the populations somewhat, although it would still prefer that the distributions have the same general shape. But let's go ahead and run the test and see how the results come out, even though I feel some concern about applying the test when the distributions are oppositely skewed.

41

To run the test enter the command **Statistic/Nonparametric tests/ Wilcoxon signed-ranks**, and then enter the names of the two variables you wish to compare. The results of this analysis are shown below, along with the command that StataQuest generated from the menu entries.

```
. signrank InstA = InstB

Test:  Equality of distributions (Wilcoxon Signed-Ranks)

Result of InstA - (InstB)
 Sum of Positive Ranks = 263
 Sum of Negative Ranks = 1012

 z-statistic   -3.62
 Prob > |z|     0.0003
```

Notice that the test prints out the sum of the positive and negative ranks, and then uses the normal approximation (z) to evaluate these two sums. The value of z is quite extreme ($z = -3.62$), with a probability under H_0 of 0.0003. Once again we would reject the equality of the means of the two instruments, this time with a test that makes somewhat less restrictive assumptions. Again, however, my earlier comment about the practical meaning of this difference continues to apply.

NOW IT'S YOUR TURN

This has been a brief description of using StataQuest to run statistical analyses addressing useful research questions. As promised, I have not covered anything close to all of the possible commands. However, I have covered enough that you should feel able to work your own problems. Do not expect that you can do so without making errors; you would be surprised if you knew how many errors I made in producing this manual. But errors are the way you learn. If something doesn't work, you play around until you find something else that does. The worst that is likely to happen is that you will make a mess of your data and have to load a new copy. (Yes, it is true that you can make your computer freeze, but just reboot and off you go—professional programmers reboot many times a day.) When all else fails, there is always your instructor.

Part II

Student Solutions Manual

with Hints and Suggestions

Prepared by

David C. Howell
and
Catherine T. Howell

Chapter 1 - Introduction
=========================

1-3   You need to think of a situation in which you would expect to see *different* behaviors in *different* contexts. A relatively small amount of alcohol can have no noticeable effect in a normal situation, but quite unpleasant effects in an emotionally charged situation.

1-4   The whole point here is what kind of conclusion you wish to draw. The entire student body would be considered a population under any circumstances in which you want to generalize *only* to that student body, and no further; for instance, when the interest is in being able to make statements about the opinions of the university's own students. When you want to generalize to a larger population (all U.S. students, for example), then your student body would be considered a sample.

1-5   The issue relates to who has an equal opportunity to be included in the sample. The students of your college are a non-random sample of U.S. students, because all U.S. students do not have an equal chance of being included.

1-6   To be a random sample, everyone must have an equal chance of being included. Not all residents are listed in the phone book, and thus not all residents have an equal chance of being included in the sample. The homeless, poor people, people with unlisted numbers, and especially women and children are underrepresented. Men and middle class families will be overrepresented.

1-8   Average, mean, median, range.

1-9   The planners of a marathon race would like to know the average times of expert, average, and novice runners so as to facilitate planning. The emphasis here is on the actual times, not on a comparison with other populations.

1-10   Is the mean weight of a group of 30-year-old women who dieted consistently as teenagers different from the mean weight of a sample of 30-year-olds who did not diet as teenagers, but matched on teenage weight? Notice that we don't really care what the mean weights are—only whether they are different.

1-12   *Measurement data*: **(a)** Number of items endorsed in a 100-point scale of attitudes concerning capital punishment. **(b)** Weight (in grams) of

45

newborn rat pups following maternal dietary restrictions. (c) Number of fatal traffic accidents in California on Labor Day weekend. Notice that we are actually measuring something, rather than sorting people into categories.

1-13 To look at performance as a function of age, we could record the ages of participants in a triathlon directly in years, or we could break the ages into the standard age clusters ranging from "Juniors" to "Masters." Think about the fact that we might do different things with these data and be asking more, or less, refined questions.

1-14 Here we need to find examples in which we want to see if differences in one variable are associated with differences in another variable. (a) Vocational counselors would be interested in the relationship between high school students' scores on a vocational interest survey in 9th grade and their performance in vocational courses in 10th through 12th grades. (b) Marital counselors might investigate the relationship between frequency of arguments and underlying need for intimacy.

1-15 Here the emphasis is on differences between groups, and not about a second variable. (a) How do the final grade point averages for low-achieving students taking courses that interested them compare to the averages of low-achieving students taking courses which didn't interest them? (b) The frequency of arguments could be compared for couples who show high and low levels of intimacy. *Note* that the same variables are involved in the answers to 1-14 and 1-15, but the approach is quite different.

1-16 We need to know more about tolerance itself. One important comparison would be to take a group that had not had morphine until the test trial, and compare their performance with a group that received morphine on all trials. Both groups would always be tested in the same context. Then any differences between them on the test trial would be a straight measure of tolerance.

Chapter 2 - Basic Concepts
=============================

2-1 *Nominal*—Brand of chocolate bars preferred. *Ordinal*—The finishing order of a group of runners. *Interval*—Prison inmates are rated from 1 to 5 on each of 20 behavioral items, producing a deviance score between 20 and 100. *Ratio*—The speed with which a person with damage to the left hemisphere can speak.

2-3 We expect speed to bear an orderly relationship to what an animal has learned about the task. If the speed on one trial is quite different from speed on adjacent trials, the implication is that speed is a poor measure of learning unless we assume that the animal's knowledge fluctuates wildly from trial to trial—an unreasonable assumption.

2-4 Speed is probably a much better index of motivation than of learning. The animal may no longer care about the food reward at the end of the alley.

2-5 Remember that independent variables are the variables we manipulate, while dependent variables are the data we collect. *Independent variables*—First grade students who attended Kindergarten versus those who did not; Expert, Average, or Novice marathon runners. *Dependent variables*—Social adjustment scores assigned by first-grade teachers; Time to run 26.2 miles.

2-6 Keep in mind what we manipulated and what we measured. "This experiment examined the latency of paw licking (dependent variable) among groups of mice who were tested for morphine tolerance in either a familiar or a novel environment (independent variable)."

2-8 Remember that discrete variables take on relatively few different values. *Discrete variables*—Number of siblings; Political party affiliation (Republican, Democrat, or Independent); Male or Female.

2-9 Hypothetical musicality data for Europeans:

(a) $X_3 = 9$; $X_5 = 10$; $X_8 = 8$ (b) $\sum X = 77$

(c) $\sum_{i=1}^{10} X_i$ This is read "Sum X_i from $i = 1$ to $i = 10$."

2-11   For the data from Exercise 2-9:

(a) $(\Sigma X)^2 = 77^2 = 5929$ [Add the scores and square the result.]

$\Sigma X^2 = 10^2 + 8^2 + ... + 7^2 = 657$ [Square the scores and then sum the results.]

Notice that these two answers are quite different.

(b) $\Sigma X/N = 77/10 = 7.7$

(c) the average, or the mean

2-13   For the data from Exercises 2-9 and 2-10:

(a) $\Sigma XY = 10(9) + 8(9) + ... + 7(2) = 460$
[Multiply the paired scores together and then sum.]

(b) $\Sigma X \Sigma Y = (77)(57) = 4389$ [Multiply the sums.]

(c)

$$\frac{\Sigma XY - \dfrac{\Sigma X \Sigma Y}{N}}{N - 1} = \frac{460 - \dfrac{4389}{10}}{9} = 2.344$$

This result will later be called the "covariance."

2-14   Still using the same data:

(a) Does $\Sigma(X + Y) = \Sigma X + \Sigma Y$?

$$\begin{aligned}\Sigma(X + Y) &= (10 + 9) + (8 + 9) + ... + (7 + 2)\\ &= 19 + 17 + ... + 9\\ &= 134\end{aligned}$$

$$\begin{aligned}\Sigma X + \Sigma Y &= 77 + 57\\ &= 134\end{aligned}$$

$134 = 134$

It doesn't matter if we add X and Y and then sum the results, or if we sum the Xs, sum the Ys, and then add those sums.

(b) Does $\Sigma XY = \Sigma X \Sigma Y$?

$$\Sigma XY = 10(9) + 8(9) + \ldots + 7(2)$$
$$= 460$$

$$\Sigma X \Sigma Y = (77)(57)$$
$$= 4389$$

$$460 \neq 4389$$

Here it makes a big difference whether we multiply X and Y before summing, or multiply their sums.

(c) Does $\Sigma CX = C \Sigma X$?

$$\Sigma CX = \Sigma 3X$$
$$= 3(10) + 3(8) + \ldots + 3(7)$$
$$= 231$$

$$C \Sigma X = 3 \Sigma X$$
$$- 3(77)$$
$$= 231$$

$$231 = 231$$

You can multiply each score by a constant and then sum, or sum and then multiply that result by the constant.

(d) Does $\Sigma X^2 = (\Sigma X)^2$?

$$\Sigma X^2 = 10^2 + 8^2 + \ldots + 7^2$$
$$= 657$$

$$(\Sigma X)^2 = 77^2$$
$$= 5929$$

$$657 \neq 5929$$

This is particularly important. The sum of a column of squared scores is very different from the square of their sum. *Remember this!!*

Chapter 3 - Displaying Data
============================

3-1 Children's recall of stories:

(a) Children's data:

"and thens"	Freq
10	1
11	1
12	1
15	3
16	4
17	6
18	10
19	7
20	7
21	3
22	2
23	2
24	1
31	1
40	1

Frequency of "And-Then" Statements

(b) The distribution is unimodal because it has only one peak. It is positively skewed because the values trail off to the right.

3-3 The problem with making a stem-and-leaf display of the data in Exercise 3-1 is that almost all the values fall on only two leaves if we use the usual 10s' digits for stems. And things aren't much better even if we double the number of stems.

Stem	Leaf
1*	012
1.	555666677777778888888889999999
2*	000000011122334
2.	
3*	1
3.	
4*	0

The best solution might be to use the units digits for stems and add HI and LO for extreme values:

Stem	Leaf
LO	0 1 2
5	555
6	6666
7	7777777
8	8888888888
9	9999999
10	0000000
11	111
12	22
13	33
14	4
HI	31 40

3-4   Adults' recall of stories:

(a) The scores for adults appear to be noticeably smaller. Adults seem to rely less strongly than do children on an "and-then..." format for recalling stories.

(b) Adults' data:

"and thens"	Frequency
1	1
3	1
4	1
5	2
7	4
8	4
9	7
10	8
11	6
12	5
13	1
14	4
15	3
16	2
17	1

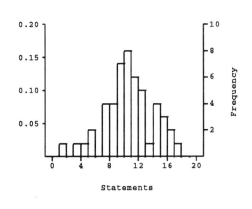

Distribution of "And-Then" Statements

(c)   Children and adults combined data:

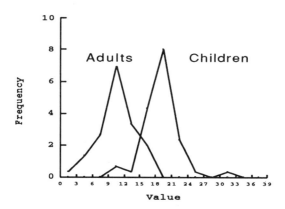

3-8   The majority of the people in the U.S. do not smoke, so I would expect the distribution of number of cigarettes smoked per day would be bimodal, with one peak at 0 cigarettes per day and another (lower) peak between one and two packs per day. The distribution would still be bimodal for a non-U.S. population, but there would most likely be fewer non-smokers.

3-11   In this question you want to focus on the differences between the two distributions. **(1)** Mexico has very many young people and very few old people, while Spain has a more even distribution. **(2)** The difference between males and females is more pronounced at most ages in Spain than it is in Mexico. **(3)** You can see the high infant mortality rate, or rapidly increasing birthrate, in Mexico.

3-12   We use HI and LO categories to keep the stem-and-leaf display from straggling off at the ends.

3-15   The figures in Exercise 3-14 support the sequential processing hypothesis because time increases with digits.

3-17   The observations are not likely to be independent because the subject is learning the task over the early trials, and later getting fatigued as the task progresses. This would cause responses closer in time to be more similar than responses farther away in time.

3-18 For subjects raised in a stable environment, there is little or no difference in immunity between High and Low Affiliation groups. However when animals are raised in an unstable environment, High Affiliation subjects showed much greater immunity than Low Affiliation subjects. Stability protects against the negative effect of low affiliation.

Chapter 4 - Central Tendency

==============================

4-1   For data in Exercise 3-1:

Mo = 18
Med = 18
Mean = $\sum X/N$ = 945/50 = 18.9

4-3   The differences in all measures of central tendency show that adults say "and then..." about half as often as children do.

4-5   For any positively skewed distribution, the mean will fall above the median because the large values will pull the mean toward them.

4-6   Invented data: 1 9 10 15 15

Mean = Median = 10
Mode = 15

4-7   Rats running a straight alley maze:

The easiest way to calculate the mean is to multiply each score (number of trials) by the corresponding frequency, and then sum the results. Divide by the total frequency. The median is just the 8th score from the top.

$$\bar{X} = \sum X/N = 320/15 = 21.33; \text{Median} = 21$$

4-11   Measures of Central Tendency for GPA:

Mo = 3.00
Med = 2.635
Mean = $\sum X/N$ = 216.15/88 = 2.46

Measures of Central Tendency for ADDSC:

Mo = 50
Med = 50
Mean = $\sum X/N$ = 4629/88 = 52.6

4-12   The numerical codes for the levels of SEX and ENGL are arbitrary—any two values could have been used. Because Sex is coded 1 and 2, with 2 representing females, the (Mean - 1) for SEX would be the *proportion* of subjects who were female. Think what the mean would be if you had exactly as many 1s and 2s. What if you had 75% 1s and 25% 2s?

4-13 The mode does not depend upon the relationships among the points on the scale, whereas the mean and median do.

Chapter 5 - Measures of Variability

===================================

5-1   For the data in Exercise 3-1:

range = 40 - 10 = 30

$$\text{Variance} = s_X^2 = \frac{\Sigma X^2 - \frac{(\Sigma X)^2}{N}}{N-1} = \frac{18851 - \frac{(945)^2}{50}}{49}$$

$$= 20.214$$

$$\text{Standard deviation} = \sqrt{s_X^2} = \sqrt{20.214} = 4.496$$

5-3   In Exercise 5-2, the standard deviation was 3.405 and the range was 16. Therefore the two standard deviations are roughly the same, although the range for the children is about twice the range for the adults. The larger range reflects two outliers in the children's scores, while the more equal standard deviations show the distributions to be otherwise similar in dispersion. It would be instructive to compare the distributions after dropping the two most extreme scores in each.

5-5   For the data in Exercise 5-2:

First we need to calculate the interval that blankets two standard deviations on either side of the mean.

The interval: $\overline{X} \pm 2s_X = 10.2 \pm 2(3.405) = 10.2 \pm 6.81$
$= 3.39$ to 17.01

From the frequency distribution in Exercise 3-4, we can see that all but two scores (1 and 3) fall in this interval. Therefore, $48/50 = 96\%$ of the scores fall in this interval.

5-8   Original data: 3 5 6 7 8 8 9 9

First we need to calculate the standard deviation.

$$s_1 = \sqrt{\dfrac{\Sigma X^2 - \dfrac{(\Sigma X)^2}{N}}{N-1}} = \sqrt{\dfrac{409 - \dfrac{(55)^2}{8}}{7}} = \sqrt{4.411} = 2.1$$

If $X_2 = CX_1$, then $s_2 = Cs_1$ and we want $s_2 = 1.00$

$s_2 = Cs_1$

$1 = C(2.1)$

$1/2.1 = C$

Therefore we must divide the original scores by 2.1:

$X_2 = \quad X_1/2.1$:

1.428 2.381 2.857 3.333 3.809 3.809 4.286 4.286

$$s_2 = \sqrt{\dfrac{92.739 - \dfrac{(26.19)^2}{8}}{7}} = \sqrt{\dfrac{6.9995}{7}} = 1$$

5-9 X_2 from Exercise 5-8:

1.428 2.381 2.857 3.333 3.809 3.809 4.286 4.286

If $X_3 = X_2 + C$, then $\overline{X}_3 = \overline{X}_2 + C$ and we want $\overline{X}_3 = 0$

$$\overline{X}_2 = \dfrac{26.19}{8} = 3.274$$

$$\overline{X}_3 = \overline{X}_2 + C$$

$0 = 3.274 + C$

$-3.274 = C$

Therefore, we want to subtract 3.274 from the X_2 scores:

$X_3 = X_2 - 3.274$:

-1.845 -0.893 -0.417 0.060 0.536 0.536 1.012 1.012

$\overline{X}_3 = (-3.155 + 3.153)/8 = -.00025 \approx 0$

5-14 (a) Variance and standard deviation for ENGG:

$$\text{Variance} = s_X^2 = \frac{\Sigma X^2 - \frac{(\Sigma X)^2}{N}}{N-1} = \frac{700 - \frac{(234)^2}{88}}{87}$$

$$= 0.894$$

$$\text{Standard deviation} = \sqrt{s_X^2} = \sqrt{0.894} = 0.946$$

(b) The variability of a set of means will be smaller than the variability of the scores from which those means were computed. In comparing GPA, we average over four or five courses and can thus balance out an extreme grade in one course with more moderate grades in others. Think about how variable a single set of quiz grades may be, but the average grades at the end of the year will be much less variable because an extreme score on one quiz will be lost in the averaging.

5-15 Adding a score equal to mean (18.9) to the data in Exercise 3-1, then recalculating the measures of variability:

range = 40 - 10 = 30

$$\text{Variance} = s_X^2 = \frac{\Sigma X^2 - \frac{(\Sigma X)^2}{N}}{N-1} = \frac{19208.21 - \frac{(963.9)^2}{51}}{50}$$

$$= 19.810$$

$$\text{Standard deviation} = \sqrt{s_X^2} = \sqrt{19.810} = 4.451$$

The range is no different from Exercise 5-1. The standard deviation is smaller than in the original data because it is an average of deviations from the mean, and we just included an additional score that had a deviation of 0.00.

5-18 Although we usually draw only one sample from the population, we would like to know that the statistics we calculate from this sample are like the statistics we would calculate if we had drawn a different random sample. If we didn't have any faith that they would be, we couldn't put much faith in the value we calculated.

5-19 We want an unbiased statistic because we want one that is a fair estimate of the corresponding population parameter—that is, does not differ systematically from that population parameter. If we thought that our statistic was not unbiased, then we would suspect that it systematically underestimated (or overestimated, as the case may be) the value we seek.

5-21 In boxplots drawn by JMP and some other software, vertical lines are drawn to cut off 2.5%, 5%, 10%, 25%, 50%, 75%, 90%, 95%, and 97.5% of the distribution. We do not see all of these lines because some of them overlap when we have few data points. The diamond marks out the mean (found at the tallest point of the diamond) and 95% confidence limits on the mean (found as the width of the diamond). Notice how much information can be contained in a small plot.

Chapter 6 - Normal Distribution
=================================

6-2   Converting specific scores from distribution in Exercise 6-1 into *z* scores:

Here we simply solve the equation for *z*, and then use the *z* tables in Appendix D to find the relevant areas.

$$z = \frac{X - \mu}{\sigma} = \frac{2.5 - 4}{1.63} = \frac{6.2 - 4}{1.63} = \frac{9 - 4}{1.63}$$

$$= -0.92 \qquad = 1.35 \qquad = 3.07$$

score (*X*)   z score

score (X)	z score	
2.5	- 0.92	18% of the distribution lies below X = 2.5
6.2	+1.35	91% of the distribution lies below X = 6.2
9.0	+3.07	99.9% of the distribution lies below X = 9.0

6-3   Errors counting shoppers in a major department store:

To solve this problem we first convert the data to standard scores using the formula for *z*, and then find the relevant areas from the *z* distribution in Appendix D.

(a

$$z = \frac{X - \mu}{\sigma}$$

$$= \frac{960 - 975}{15} = \frac{-15}{15} = -1 \text{ Between } -1 \text{ and } \mu \text{ lie } .3413$$

$$= \frac{990 - 975}{15} = \frac{+15}{15} = +1 \text{ Between } +1 \text{ and } \mu \text{ lie } \underline{.3413}$$

Total .   6826

Therefore, approximately 68% of the scores are found between 960 and 990.

(b) $975 = \mu$, therefore, 50% of the scores lie below 975

(c) .5000 lie below 975
.3413 lie between 975 and 990
.8413 (or 84%) lie below 990

6-4 Using the data in Exercise 6-3:

First we need to find those points than exceeded by the highest (and lowest) 25% of the scores. Diagram the middle 50% if this is not clear.

(a) From Appendix D:

z score	area between z and mean	
.67	.2486	
.6745	.2500	<==== [interpolation from
.68	.2517·	Appendix D]

Therefore, $z = \pm.6745$ encompasses middle 50%

$$z = \frac{X - \mu}{\sigma}$$

$$\pm 0.6745 = \frac{X - 975}{15}$$

$$X = 985.12 \text{ and } 964.88$$

Therefore, 50% of the scores lie between counts of 965 and 985.

(b) 75% of the counts would be less than 986 because we just calculated the middle 50%, 25% of which lies on either side of the mean. Since 50% lies below the mean, $50 + 25 = 75\%$ lies below 986.

(c) What scores would 95% of the counts lie between?

First we need to find from Appendix D what z score cuts off the top 2.5% and what z score cuts off the bottom 2.5%. Together these cut off the extreme 5%. From Appendix D these values are -1.96 and +1.96. We then insert these in the z formula and solve for X.

$$z = \frac{X - \mu}{\sigma} \qquad z_{.95} = \pm 1.96$$

$$\pm 1.96 = \frac{X - 975}{15}$$

$$X = 945.6 \text{ and } 1004.4$$

95% of the counts would lie between 946 and 1004.

6-5   The supervisor's count of shoppers:

To solve this, we need to find how extreme is the supervisor's score. We calculate his z score and look the answer up in Appendix D.

$$z = \frac{X - \mu}{\sigma}$$

$$= \frac{950 - 975}{15}$$

$$= -1.67$$

The area outside $z = \pm 1.67 = 2(.0475) = .095$, therefore, 9.5% of the time scores will be at least this extreme.

6-6   **(a)** Sketch:

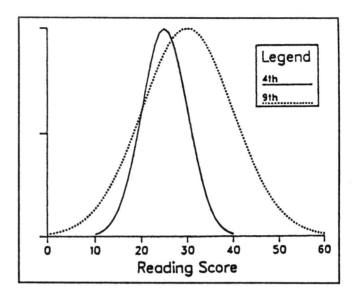

(b)   The percentage of 4th graders better than the average ninth grader is just the percentage of fourth graders with a score greater than 30.

$$z = \frac{X - \mu}{\sigma}$$

$$= \frac{30 - 25}{5}$$

$$= +1.00$$

The smaller portion for $z = +1.00$ is .1587. Therefore, approximately 16% of the 4th graders score better than the average 9th grader.

(c)

$$z = \frac{X - \mu}{\sigma}$$

$$= \frac{25 - 30}{10}$$

$$= -0.50$$

The smaller portion for $z = -.5$ is .3085, therefore approximately 31% of the 9th graders score worse than the average 4th grader.

6-7 They would be equal when the two distributions have the same standard deviation.

6-8 Diagnostically meaningful cutoff:

We first need to find that z score cutting off the lowest 10%, and then we need to convert that standard score (z) to a raw score.

$$z = \frac{X - \mu}{\sigma}$$

$$-1.2817 = \frac{X - 150}{30}$$

$$111.549 = X$$

z score	area above z
1.28	.1003
1.2817	.1000
1.29	.0985

The diagnostically meaningful cutoff is 111.549.

6-10 Introductory psychology students checking seatbelt usage:

(a) **Seat Belt Use**

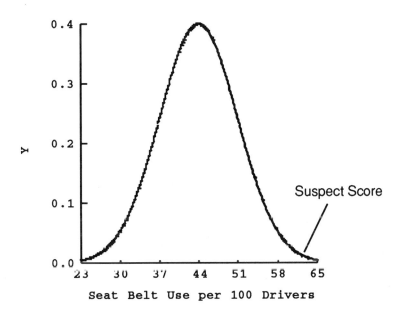

Seat Belt Use per 100 Drivers

(b) To find how unusual that score would be, we just convert it to a z score and then find the probability associated with that z score.

$$z = \frac{X - \mu}{\sigma} = \frac{62 - 44}{7} = 2.57; \; p = .0051$$

A count this high (or higher) would occur by chance only 0.5% of the time. The suspicion is that he just made up a number.

6-11 Transforming scores on diagnostic test for language problems:

X_1 = original scores: $\mu_1 = 48$ $\sigma_1 = 7$
X_2 = transformed scores: $\mu_2 = 80$ $\sigma_2 = 10$

We know that if we divide by a constant we will divide the standard deviation by that constant. We therefore need to know the divisor to get a standard deviation of 10.

$$\sigma_2 = \sigma_1/C$$

$$10 = 7/C$$

$$C = .7$$

Therefore, to transform the original standard deviation from 7 to 10, we need to divide the original scores by .7. But, dividing the original scores by .7 also divides their mean by .7.

$$\bar{X}_2 = \bar{X}_1/.7$$

$$= 48/.7 = 68.57$$

We want to raise the mean to 80. Because $80 - 68.57 = 11.43$, we need to add 11.43 to each score.

$$X_2 = X_1/.7 + 11.43 \quad \text{[This formula summarizes the whole process]}$$

6-12 Skewed distribution of diagnostic test for language problems:

(a) Diagram:

Language Problems

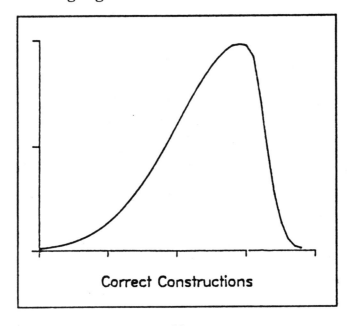

Correct Constructions

(b) To find the cutoff for the bottom 10% if the distribution is not normal, simply count up from the bottom until you find the lowest 10%. This is the empirical approach.

6-13   October, 1981, GRE, all people taking the exam had a mean of 489 and a standard deviation of 126. First convert 600 to a z score, and then find the area of the larger portion.

$$z = \frac{X - \mu}{\sigma}$$

$$= \frac{600 - 489}{126}$$

$$= .88 \qquad p(\text{larger portion}) = .81$$

A GRE score of 600 would correspond to the 81st percentile.

6-16   Percentiles are dependent upon the reference group. As a group, the seniors and non-enrolled college graduates did better on the GRE than the average of all people taking the exam. A person receiving a given score, therefore, did better (scored at a higher percentile) when compared to all people taking the exam than when compared only to the seniors and nonenrolled college graduates taking the exam.

6-18   Diagnostically meaningful cutoff for Behavior Problem scores:

We need to find the z score that cuts off the highest 2%. From Appendix D, by interpolation, that is 2.054. We then convert that z score to a raw score by solving for X.

z score	p
2.05	.9798
2.054	.9800
2.06	.9803

$$z = \frac{X - \overline{X}}{s}$$

$$2.054 = \frac{X - 50}{10}$$

$$70.54 = X = \text{cutoff}$$

Chapter 7 - Probability
=========================

7-1 (**a**) *Analytic*—If two tennis players are exactly equally skillful so that the outcome of their match is random, the probability is .50 that Player A will win their upcoming match. Notice that this statement makes no reference to past outcomes of their matches.

(**b**) *Relative frequency*—If in past matches Player A has beaten Player B on 13 of the 17 occasions, then Player A has a probability of $13/17 = .76$ of winning their upcoming match. Notice that this statement is based solely on past performance.

(**c**) *Subjective*—Player A's coach feels that she has a probability of .90 of winning her upcoming match with Player B. This is a purely subjective statement with no explicit reference to an analysis of the situation or past experience.

7-2 1000 tickets sold for the local fire department lottery:

(**a**) There are 1000 tickets, of which only one can be a winner. Thus, $p = 1/1000 = .001$ that you will win.

(**b**) Each of your brother's two tickets has a 1 in a 1000 chance of winning. Because he has two tickets, he has two chances of winning. Thus, $p = 2/1000 = .002$ that your brother will win.

(**c**) Here we just sum the probabilities: $p = .001 + .002 = .003$ that one or the other of you will win. [uses additive law]

7-3 Only 10 tickets sold for the local fire department lottery:

(**a**) After the first prize is drawn, there are only 9 competing tickets remaining. Thus, $p = 1/9 = .111$ that you will win 2nd prize given that you don't win 1st.

(**b**) Here you multiply the probability that he will come in first times the probability that you will come in second: $p = (2/10)(1/9) = (.20)(.111) = .022$ that he will win 1st and you 2nd. [We are using the multiplicative law]

(c) This is the reverse of (b).

$p = (1/10)(2/9) = (.10)(.22) = .022$ that you will win 1st and he 2nd. [We again use the multiplicative law]

(d) We just add the two probabilities computed above.
probability that you are 1st and he 2nd: $p = .022$
probability that he is 1st and you 2nd: $p = .022$
Therefore p(that you and he will be 1st and 2nd): $p = .044$
[Here we use the additive law]

7-4   Joint probabilities were involved in Exercise 7-3(b) and (c) and when we combined those results in (d). We are talking about the probability that more than one outcome will occur *at the same time*.

7-5   Conditional probabilities were involved in Exercise 7-3(a). Notice the word "given" in that question.

7-8   If mothers' and infants' looking behaviors are independent, the probability that they will look at each other at the same time can be obtained by multiplication.

$p = (2/24)(3/24) = (.083)(.125) = .01$

[We use the multiplicative law for joint occurrence of independent events]

7-10   A flier that contains a message asking the person to dispose of it properly has a higher probability of being found in the trash (.045) than we would expect if the message and disposal were independent events (.033). This difference is small, but the probabilities are based on many observations, and are thus quite stable.

7-11   A continuous distribution for which we care about the probability of an observation's falling within some specified interval is exemplified by the probability that your baby will be born on its due date. (Here we have an interval of 24 hours.)

7-12   The continuous distribution of children's learning abilities is often treated as discrete by school systems that divide children into those needing special education versus those who should attend regular classes. Often they further divide the regular classes into fast, average, and slow tracks.

7-14 Randomly chosen graduate school applicants from above 80th percentile:

> Ten of the 1000 applicants with unknown ratings are admitted, so $p = 10/1000 = .01$

We have no additional information for calculating p.

7-15 Using the data from Exercise 7-14:

> **(a)** If she has the highest rating, she will automatically fall in the pool from which successful applicants are drawn. But she still has to compete with the other applicants in that pool. Only 20%, or 200 applicants, will fall at or above the 80th percentile, and 10 of these will be chosen. Therefore, $p = 10/200 = .05$ that she will be admitted given that she falls in this rating category.

> **(b)** No one below the 80th percentile will be admitted; therefore $p = .00$.

7-16 Here we need to calculate the z score corresponding to 50, and then evaluate the probability of that z score.

ADDSC: $\bar{X} = 52.6$ $s = 12.42$

$$z = \frac{50 - 52.6}{12.42} = -0.21 \quad p(\text{larger portion}) = .5832$$

7-19 If ADDSC is predictive of later school dropouts, then the probability of dropping out should be higher for those with high ADDSC scores than for people in general. Compare the probability of dropping out of school, ignoring the ADDSC score, with the conditional probability of dropping out given that ADDSC in elementary school exceeded some value (e.g., 66).

Chapter 8 - Hypothesis Testing

8-1   Was last night's game an NHL hockey game?

(a) Null hypothesis: The game was actually an NHL hockey game.

(b) On the basis of that null hypothesis I expected, from previous experience with hockey games, that each team would earn somewhere between 0 and 6 points. I then looked at the actual points and concluded that they were way out of line with what I would expect if this were an NHL hockey game. I therefore rejected the null hypothesis.

8-2   Am I overcharged at lunch?

(a) Sketch:

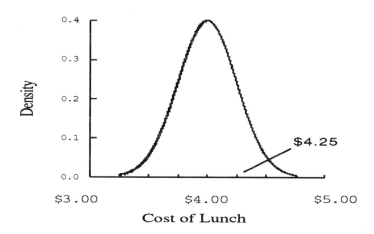

(b) No, $4.25 is a common observation, as can be seen in the figure above.

(c) I set up the null hypothesis that I was charged correctly. If that hypothesis were true, I would expect to receive about $1.00 in change, give or take a quarter or so. The change that I received was in line with that expectation, and therefore I have no basis for rejecting H_0.

71

8-3   Type I errors involve rejecting a true null hypothesis. A Type I error would be concluding that I had been shortchanged when in fact I had not.

8-5   The critical value would be that amount of change below which I would decide that I had been shortchanged. The rejection region would be all amounts less than the critical value—i.e., all amounts that would lead to rejection of H_0.

8-7   Was the son of the member of the Board of Trustees fairly admitted to graduate school? To answer this we need to calculate the probability that an admitted student would have a score of 490. Convert 490 to a z score, and look that z score up in Appendix D.

$$\bar{X} = 650 \qquad s = 50$$

z score	p
3.00	.0013
3.20	.0007
3.25	.0006

$$z = \frac{490 - 650}{50}$$

$$= -3.2$$

The probability that a student drawn at random from those properly admitted would have a GRE score as low as 490 is only .0007. I suspect that the fact that his mother was a member of the board played a role in his admission.

8-8   The standard deviation is smaller than the standard deviation of GRE scores in general because we have restricted our sample to admitted students, i.e., a high-scoring sample.

8-10   The sampling distribution of a statistic is the distribution of that statistic over repeated samples. I would draw a very large number of samples. For each sample I would calculate the mode, the range, and their ratio (M). I would then plot the resulting value of M.

8-11 M is called a test statistic—it is a statistic used to test hypotheses.

8-13   The alternative hypothesis is the opposite of the null hypothesis. It is the hypothesis that this student was sampled from a population of students whose mean is not equal to 650.

8-14   Sampling error is variability in a statistic from sample to sample which is due to chance—i.e., which is due to which particular observations happened to be included in the sample.

8-16 If α were to decrease, the rejection region would decrease. This would mean that β would increase and power would decrease. Refer to Figure 8.4.

======================

9-2   Correlation between Y and X_1 in 9-1:

$N = 10$ $\Sigma X_1 Y = 3106.54$

$\Sigma X_1 = 460$ $\Sigma Y = 67$

$\Sigma X_1{}^2 = 21515.98$ $\Sigma Y^2 = 453.28$

$$r = \frac{N\Sigma XY - \Sigma X \Sigma Y}{\sqrt{(N\Sigma X^2 - (\Sigma X)^2)(N\Sigma Y^2 - (\Sigma Y)^2)}}$$

$$= \frac{10(3106.54) - (460)(67)}{\sqrt{(10(21515.98) - (460)^2)(10(453.28) - (67)^2)}}$$

$$= .62$$

9-3   Correlation between percentage of LBW infants (Y) and percentage of births to unmarried mothers(X_2) in Vermont Health Planning Districts:

$N = 10$ $\Sigma X_2 Y = 689.62$

$\Sigma X_2 = 102.5$ $\Sigma Y = 67$

$\Sigma X_2{}^2 = 1066.35$ $\Sigma Y^2 = 453.28$

$$r = \frac{N\Sigma XY - \Sigma X \Sigma Y}{\sqrt{(N\Sigma X^2 - (\Sigma X)^2)(N\Sigma Y^2 - (\Sigma Y)^2)}}$$

$$= \frac{10(689.62) - (102.5)(67)}{\sqrt{(10(1066.35) - (102.5)^2)(10(453.28) - (67)^2)}}$$

$$= .35$$

9 - 7   Three sets of data:

Set 1

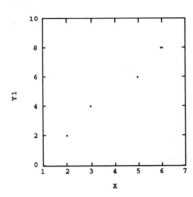

Set 2

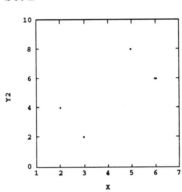

Set 3

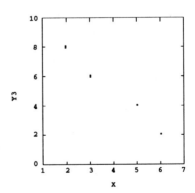

(a) Covariances using definitional formula:

$$\text{cov}_{XY} = \frac{\Sigma(X - \overline{X})(Y - \overline{Y})}{N - 1}$$

	Set 1				Set 2				Set 3		
X	X-X̄	Y	Y-Ȳ	X	X-X̄	Y	Y-Ȳ	X	X-X̄	Y	Y-Ȳ
2	-2	2	-3	2	-2	4	-1	2	-2	8	3
3	-1	4	-1	3	-1	2	-3	3	-1	6	1
5	1	6	1	5	1	8	3	5	1	4	-1
6	2	8	3	6	2	6	1	6	2	2	-3

$\Sigma = 16 \qquad 20 \qquad\qquad 16 \qquad\qquad 20 \qquad\qquad 16 \qquad\qquad 20$

$\overline{X} = 4 \qquad\quad 5 \qquad\qquad 4 \qquad\qquad 5 \qquad\qquad 4 \qquad\qquad 5$

$\Sigma(X - \overline{X})(Y - \overline{Y}) = 14 \qquad\qquad\qquad 10 \qquad\qquad\qquad -14$

$\Sigma X^2 = 74 \quad 120 \qquad 74 \qquad\qquad 120 \qquad\qquad 74 \qquad\qquad 120$

$\Sigma XY = \qquad 94 \qquad\qquad\qquad 90 \qquad\qquad\qquad\qquad 66$

$\text{cov}_{XY} = 14/3 = 4.67 \qquad = 10/3 = 3.33 \qquad = -14/3 = -4.67$

(b) Covariances using computational formula:

$$\text{cov}_{XY} = \frac{\Sigma(X - \overline{X})\Sigma(Y - \overline{Y})}{N - 1}$$

$$= \frac{94 - \dfrac{16(20)}{4}}{3} = 4.67$$

$$= \frac{90 - \dfrac{16(20)}{4}}{3} = 3.33$$

$$= \frac{66 - \dfrac{16(20)}{4}}{3} = -4.67$$

76

9-8   Correlations for the three data sets in Exercise 9-7:

(a)

$$r = \frac{N\Sigma XY - \Sigma X \Sigma Y}{\sqrt{(N\Sigma X^2 - (\Sigma X)^2)(N\Sigma Y^2 - (\Sigma Y)^2)}}$$

$$\text{Set 1: } = \frac{4(94) - 16(20)}{\sqrt{(4(74) - (16)^2)(4(120) - (20)^2)}} = .99$$

$$\text{Set 2: } = \frac{4(90) - 16(20)}{\sqrt{(4(74) - (16)^2)(4(120) - (20)^2)}} = .71$$

$$\text{Set 3: } = \frac{4(66) - 16(20)}{\sqrt{(4(74) - (16)^2)(4(120) - (20)^2)}} = -.99$$

(b) The easiest way to determine how to arrange the data is by trial and error. Three arrangements of Y will result in the lowest possible positive correlation:

   2 8 6 4 or   6 4 2 8   or   6 2 8 4 $[r = .14]$

9-9   Correlation of voluntary homework problems (X) and final course grade (Y):

(a) Scatter plot:

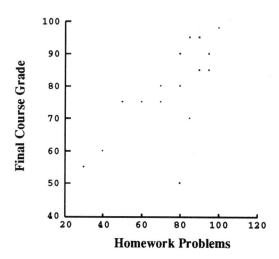

Homework Problems and Course Grade

(b) Correlation using formula involving covariance and standard deviations.

$N = 20$ $\Sigma XY = 112,350$

$\Sigma X = 1410$ $\Sigma Y = 1533$

$\Sigma X^2 = 108,400$ $\Sigma Y^2 = 121,229$

$$\text{cov}_{XY} = \frac{\Sigma XY - \dfrac{\Sigma X \Sigma Y}{N}}{N-1}$$

$$= \frac{112,350 - \dfrac{(1410)(1533)}{20}}{19}$$

$$= 224.921$$

$$s_X = 21.758$$

$$s_Y = 14.001$$

$$r = \frac{\text{cov}_{XY}}{s_X s_Y} = \frac{224.921}{(21.758)(14.001)} = .738 = .74$$

(c) Test of significance of r:

Here we compare the obtained r against the tabled value in Appendix D.2. In that table we find that any r greater than $\pm$ .444 is significantly different from 0.

(d) The correlation of .74 is significant. We can conclude that solving voluntary homework problems is related to final course grade.

9-10 I recommend doing these calculations by computer software, but I will run the correlation between I-131 levels and the decline in verbal scores by hand for demonstration purposes. The decline for verbal SAT scores from 1978 to 1979 would be calculated by V78 – V77 (the scores for tests taken in 1978-79 minus the scores for tests taken in 1977–78).

(I)	(V)	(M)
I-131	V78-V77	M78-M77

*104	-6	-7
12	-7	-5
37	-5	-1
13	1	7
15	-4	-3
21	-3	-4
32	-3	-9
12	-2	-1
25	-8	-3
38	-1	0
33	-1	-2
59	2	-2
22	1	1
24	-5	-2
22	-2	-2
30	-3	-3
43	0	-1
58	-4	-2
40	-6	-8
20	-2	-3
22	0	1
21	1	-3
28	-5	-2
35	-2	-2
48	3	-5
27	-3	-3
36	-1	-3
23	-1	-4
38	-7	-4
* 87	-9	-26
23	0	-1
43	-3	0
39	-3	-5
55	-10	-10
53	3	0

$N = 35$

$\Sigma I = 1238 \qquad \Sigma I^2 = 57166$

$\Sigma V = -95 \qquad \Sigma V^2 = 621$

$\Sigma M = -117 \qquad \Sigma M^2 = 1239$

$\Sigma IV = -3891 \qquad \Sigma IM = -5991$

$$\text{cov}_{IV} = \frac{\Sigma IV - \dfrac{\Sigma I \Sigma V}{N}}{N-1}$$

$$= \frac{-3891 - \dfrac{(1238)(-95)}{35}}{34}$$

$$= -15.609$$

$$\text{cov}_{IM} = \frac{\Sigma IM - \dfrac{\Sigma I \Sigma M}{N}}{N-1}$$

$$= \frac{-5991 - \dfrac{(1238)(-117)}{35}}{34}$$

$$= -54.487$$

$s = 19.835$

$s_V = 3.268$

$s_M = 4.994$

$$r = \frac{\text{cov}_{XY}}{s_X s_Y} = \frac{-15.609}{(19.835)(3.268)} = -.24$$

$$r_{IM} = \frac{\text{cov}_{IM}}{s_I s_M} = \frac{-54.487}{(19.835)(4.994)} = -.55$$

The correlation between I131 levels and Math SAT scores is –.55. The larger correlation, then, is with Math and not Verbal SAT as reported by Sternglass and Bell (1983).

9-13 In computing correlations each data point (state) counts equally, but because some data points are based on very small numbers of students, the influence of these states is overrepresented in the correlations relative to the state's population.

9-18 Ranked data from Exercise 9-1 (Y versus X_1):

District	Y	X_1	X_2	$D = Y - X_1$	$D = Y - X_2$
1	9	7	9	2	0
2	3	2	1	1	2
3	2	3.5	5	-1.5	-3
4	7.5	10	6.5	-2.5	1
5	6	5	6.5	1	-0.5
6	10	9	10	1	0
7	5	6	4	-1	1
8	1	3.5	8	-2.5	-7
9	7.5	8	2.5	-0.5	5
10	4	1	2.5	3	1.5

$\Sigma X =$ 55   55   55   0   0

$\Sigma X^2 =$ 384.5   384.5   384   32   91.5

$\Sigma X_1 Y =$ 368.5

$\Sigma X_2 Y =$ 338.5

Spearman's formula: Pearson's formula

(Not given in text)

$$r_s = 1 - \frac{6\Sigma D^2}{N(N^2 - 1)} \qquad r = \frac{N\Sigma XY - \Sigma X \Sigma Y}{\sqrt{(N\Sigma X^2 - (\Sigma X)^2)(N\Sigma Y^2 - (\Sigma Y)^2)}}$$

$$= 1 - \frac{6(32)}{10(10^2 - 1)} \qquad r = \frac{10(368.5) - 55(55)}{\sqrt{(10(384.5) - (55)^2)(10(384.5) - (55)^2)}}$$

$$= .806 \qquad\qquad\qquad = .805$$

The two answers differ slightly because no correction for tied ranks was used to obtain r_s using Spearman's formula (none is needed when Pearson's formula is used). I showed the calculations using a special formula not given in the text to illustrate that there is nothing special about the results of that formula.

9-20   Yes. The coefficient (r) would still tell you how well a straight line fits, even if you think that a curved line would fit better. Often the fit of a straight line is sufficiently good for our purposes. As a good illustration, in the section of the manual dealing with StataQuest, I used the example of the relationship between two measures of air quality. Although there is a distinct curvilinear relationship between those measures, a straight line fits the data very well.

9-21   When we say that a correlation coefficient is reliable we mean that if we drew repeated samples from the same population, the correlation coefficients for those samples would be of the same general magnitude. Correlations based on small samples are often unreliable because unusual data points which may occur in one sample but not in others can have an important influence on the correlation coefficient.

Chapter 10 - Regression
========================

10-1   Regression equation predicting Y from X_1 from Exercise 9-1:

We first need to calculate the covariance and the variance of X (shown on the right). These then supply the elements of the formulae to the left.

$$b = \frac{cov_{XY}}{s_X^2}$$

$$cov_{XY} = \frac{\sum XY - \frac{\sum X \sum Y}{N}}{N - 1}$$

$$= \frac{2.727}{39.553}$$

$$= \frac{3106.54 - \frac{460(67)}{10}}{9} = 2.727$$

$$= 0.0689$$

$$a = \frac{\sum Y - b\sum X}{N}$$

$$s_x^2 = \frac{\sum X^2 - \frac{(\sum X)^2}{N}}{N - 1}$$

$$= \frac{67 - .0689(460)}{10}$$

$$= \frac{21515.98 - \frac{460^2}{10}}{9} = 39.553$$

$$= 3.53$$

$$Y = bX + a$$
$$= .069X + 3.53$$

10-2   Standard error of estimate for regression equation in Exercise 10-1:

Here we need to calculate the standard deviation of Y and obtain r from a previous calculation. We then put the two together to obtain the standard error of estimate.

$$N = 10 \quad r = .62 \quad \text{[Calculated in Exercise 9-2]}$$

$$s_{Y-\hat{Y}} = s_Y \sqrt{(1 - r^2)\frac{N-1}{N-2}} \qquad s_Y = \sqrt{\frac{\Sigma Y^2 - \dfrac{(\Sigma Y)^2}{N}}{N-1}}$$

$$= .6976\sqrt{(1 - .62)^2(9/8)} \qquad = \sqrt{\frac{453.28 - \dfrac{67^2}{10}}{9}}$$

$$= .5805 \qquad\qquad = .6976$$

10-3   If high-risk fertility rate in Exercise 9-1 jumped to 70, we could predict the incidence of low birthweight simply by inserting 70 in the regression equation.

$$= bX + a$$

$$= .069(70) + 3.53$$

$$= 8.36 \text{ would be the predicted percentage of LBW infants born.}$$

10-5   Regression equation for predicting final grade (Y) from number of homework problems completed (X) in Exercise 9-9:

$$\text{cov}_{XY} = \frac{\Sigma XY - \dfrac{\Sigma X \Sigma Y}{N}}{N-1} = \frac{112350 - \dfrac{1410(1533)}{20}}{19} = 244.92$$

$$s_X^2 = \frac{\Sigma X^2 - \dfrac{(\Sigma X)^2}{N}}{N-1} = \frac{108400 - \dfrac{1410^2}{20}}{19} = 473.42$$

$$b = \frac{\text{cov}_{XY}}{s_X^2} = \frac{224.92}{473.42} = 0.475$$

$$a = \frac{\Sigma Y - b\Sigma X}{N} = \frac{1533 - 0.475(1410)}{20} = 43.16$$

$$\hat{Y} = bX + a = 0.475X + 43.16$$

10-7   From Table 10-2:

Here we simply insert $X = 45$ in our regression equation and solve for $\hat{Y}$.

Regression equation: $\hat{Y} = 0.7831X + 73.891$

If Stress $(X) = 45$: $= 0.7831(45) + 73.891$

Predicted Symptom Score: $= 109.13$

10-10   Predicting mean 1978 SAT Math from SAT Verbal:

$$b = \frac{\text{cov}_{MV}}{s_V^2} \qquad \text{cov}_{MV} = \frac{\Sigma MV - \dfrac{\Sigma M \Sigma V}{N}}{N \quad 1}$$

$$= \frac{1256.98}{1196.68} \qquad = \frac{9873432 - \dfrac{19699(21437)}{43}}{42} = 1256.98$$

$$= 1.05$$

$$a = \frac{\Sigma M - b\Sigma V}{N} \qquad s_v^2 = \frac{\Sigma V^2 - \dfrac{(\Sigma V)^2}{N}}{N - 1}$$

$$= \frac{21437 - 1.05(19699)}{43} \qquad = \frac{50718.676 - \dfrac{19699^2}{43}}{42} = 1196.68$$

$$= 17.33$$

$$\hat{Y} = bV + a$$
$$= 1.05V + 17.33$$

10-11   A 1-unit difference in the SAT Verbal score is associated with a 1.05-unit difference in the predicted SAT Math score. The intercept has no interpretable meaning because a Verbal score of 0 is not a legitimate value. Notice that this does *not* say that if you were to increase your own Verbal SAT by one point you would increase your Math SAT accordingly. We are not speaking about causal relationships.

10-14   Predict GPA (*Y*) from ADDSC (*X*):

This solution is straight-forward and is similar to previous problems. We simply calculate the covariance of GPA and ADDSC and use the variance of ADDSC that we calculated earlier.

$$b = \frac{\text{cov}_{XY}}{s_X^2} \qquad N = 88 \quad \Sigma X = 4629 \qquad \Sigma Y = 216.15$$

$$= \frac{-6.580}{154.431} \qquad \Sigma XY = 10797.53$$

$$= -.0426 \qquad s_X = 12.4222 \quad s_X^2 = 154.431$$

$$a = \frac{\Sigma Y - b\Sigma X}{N} \qquad \text{cov}_{XY} = \frac{\Sigma XY - \dfrac{\Sigma X \Sigma Y}{N}}{N - 1}$$

$$= 4.699 \qquad = \frac{10797.53 - \dfrac{4629(216.15)}{88}}{87}$$

$$\hat{Y} = bX + a \qquad = -6.580$$

$$= -.0426 + 4.699$$

10-16   The best estimate of starting salary for faculty is $28,000. For every additional year of service, salary increases by $900 on average. For administrative staff the best estimate of starting salary is $18,000, but every year of additional service increases the salary by an average of $1500. They will be approximately equal after 16 2/3 years of service. This last is obtained by setting the two equations equal to each other and solving for *X*. (This is something you did frequently in high school, but may have forgotten. If two things are equal, then we can set their equations equal to each other. We then simplify the equations to calculate *X*. This is the value of *X* (*Years*) when the two sides are equal).

$$0.9X + 28 = 1.5X + 18$$
$$0.9X - 1.5X = 18 - 28$$
$$-0.6X = -10$$
$$X = \frac{-10}{-0.6} = 16.67$$

You can verify this answer by inserting it in both equations and seeing that they come out to the same result (43). This result is the individual's salary (in thousands of dollars).

Chapter 11 - Multiple Regression

===================================

11-1   Predicting Quality of Life:

(**a**)   A regression coefficient represents the degree to which $\hat{Y}$ will change for a 1-unit change in that predictor variable, assuming that all other variables are held constant. Thus, with all other variables held constant, a difference of +1 degree in Temperature is associated with a difference of −.01 in perceived Quality of Life. A difference of $1000 in median Income, again with all other variables held constant, is associated with a +.05 difference in perceived Quality of Life. A similar interpretation applies to b_3 and b_4. Since values of 0 cannot reasonably occur for all predictors, the intercept has no meaningful interpretation here.

(**b**) Here we simply substitute the values of the predictors for their algebraic representation and solve the equation.

$$\hat{Y} = 5.37 - .01(55) + .05(12) + .003(500) - .01(200) = 4.92$$

(**c**) The only difference in this equation would be the amount spent on social services.

$$\hat{Y} = 5.37 - .01(55) + .05(12) + .003(100) - .01(200) = 3.72$$

Notice that our prediction is 1.20 units lower due to the $400 difference in spending on social services.

11-2   Prediction of job satisfaction:

(**a**)   Yes, we are predicting at better-than-chance levels. The F for the test on the multiple correlation is 16.57 on 4 and 70 df, which is significant at $p = .000$.

(**b**) The regression equation is written using the entries from the column headed "COEFFICIENT."

$$\hat{Y} = 0.605\text{Respon} - 0.334\text{NumSup} + 0.486\text{Envir} + 0.070\text{Yrs} + 1.669$$

(**c**)   The multiple correlation is 0.6974.

11-3   With all four predictor variables in the equation, the only one to be significant at $p < .05$ is Years of Service. This coefficient had a $t = 5.402$, with an associated probability of 0.000 to three decimal places. (This is not to say that the other variables would not be significant if Yrs were dropped from the equation.)

11-4   When predictors are highly correlated among themselves, we have less faith in the stability of our solution. We look to tolerance as a way of gaging this interdependence of the predictors. Respon and NumSup are highly correlated with the other predictors taken as a set (For Respon predicted from the other variables, $1 - R^2 = .26$. Therefore $R^2 = .74$, and $R = .86$.) Envir is less highly correlated with the other predictors, whereas Years of Service is largely independent of the others.

11-5   Yrs is the only variable to add much information that is not contained in the other variables. This may partly explain why it contributes to the prediction far more than do the others.

Chapter 12 - One-Sample *t* Test
================================

12-6   North Dakota verbal SAT: $\overline{X} = 525$

(**a**) Is a mean of 525 consistent with SAT mean of 500 and standard deviation of 100? To solve this we convert 525 to a *z* score and then look up the probability of a *z* as extreme as the one we have.

$$z = \frac{\overline{X} - \mu}{\sigma_{\overline{X}}} = \frac{525 - 500}{\frac{100}{\sqrt{238}}} = 3.86$$

The probability of a *z* as extreme as $\pm 3.86 = 2(.0001) = .0002$, so we would reject the hypothesis that the SAT has a mean of 500 and a standard deviation of 100. A mean that extreme would only occur 2 times out of every 10,000 if the true population mean and standard deviation are 500 and 100.

(**b**) Using a one-tailed test ($\overline{X} < 500$), the null hypothesis would not have been rejected because the difference (although significant by a two-tailed test), was in the unexpected direction.

(**c**)   You could either conclude that the North Dakota students are not representative of students in general, or you could conclude that our assumptions about the mean and standard deviation in the U.S. population were in error to begin with.

12-7   The data don't address the issue because: (1) It is not a random sample; (2) We have no definition of what is meant by "a terrible state" nor whether SAT scores measure it. The data speak only about how North Dakota compares to the general population.

12-8   Arizona math SAT: $\overline{X} = 524$

$$z = \frac{\overline{X} - \mu}{\sigma_{\overline{X}}} = \frac{524 - 500}{\frac{100}{\sqrt{2345}}} = 11.62 \quad p = .0000$$

We would reject H_0 because a value of z as extreme as 11.62 is very unlikely when the null hypothesis is true.

12-10 The mean verbal GRE of 5701 college seniors and nonenrolled college graduates in the biological sciences = 503, with $s = 104$. We want to compare this mean to a population mean of 500. Since we are using the sample variance ($= 104^2 = 10816$), we will solve for t.

$$t = \frac{\overline{X} - \mu}{\sqrt{\dfrac{s^2}{N}}} = \frac{503 - 500}{\sqrt{\dfrac{10816}{5701}}} = 2.18$$

$t_{.025}(5700) = \pm 1.96 < 2.18$ We reject H_0.

The critical value of t (± 1.96) is the same as z's critical value because we have 5700 degrees of freedom. See Figure 12.5.

12-12 No, it would not have made sense to run a one-tailed test for Exercise 12-10 because we want to reject H_0 whenever $\mu \neq 500$, regardless of the direction of the difference.

12-13 In this case it is not an important finding because the difference is so small. Even if $\mu = 503$ instead of 500, it makes no particular difference to anyone—it certainly does not qualify as a sign of major improvement in GRE scores, especially since it is based on a selected sample.

12-14 For women: $\overline{X} = 24.1$ $s^2 = 38.77$

Here we need to compare the mean salary of a sample of women against the mean salary of all males (whom we will treat as a population because we don't have a larger outside group that is relevant.)

$$t = \frac{\overline{X} - \mu}{\sqrt{\dfrac{s^2}{N}}} = \frac{24.1 - 27}{\sqrt{\dfrac{38.77}{10}}} = -1.47$$

$t_{.025}(9) = \pm 2.26 > -1.47$

Do not reject H_0. We will conclude that the mean salary of our sample is not significantly less than the population mean. (Here we have only 10 observations, so the chance of rejecting the null hypothesis, even if it is false, was not high to begin with.)

12-16   For the data in Exercise 12-6:

Here we need to find an interval that is 1.96 standard errors on either side of the sample mean. We use 1.96, because $z = \pm 1.96$ cuts off the lowest and highest 2.5% of the distribution.

$$CI_{.95} = \bar{X} \pm z_{.025}(\sigma_X)$$

$$= 525 \pm (1.96)(100/\sqrt{238})$$

$$= 525 \pm 12.7$$

$$512.3 \le \mu \le 537.7$$

12-18   In Exercise 12-16 we knew σ instead of s, so we used z. In Exercise 12-17 we knew s and therefore used t. The critical value in both cases was 1.96 because, with the large number of df in Exercise 12-17 (5700), the t distribution is approximated closely by the z distribution.

12-19   IQs for females in Data Set:

$$\bar{X} = 101.82 \quad s = 12.68 \quad N = 33$$

$$t = \frac{\bar{X} - \mu}{\sqrt{\dfrac{s^2}{N}}} = \frac{101.82 - 100}{\sqrt{\dfrac{12.68^2}{33}}} = 0.82$$

$$[t_{.025}(32) = \pm 2.04]$$

Do not reject H_0. The mean IQ score for female students in not reliably different from 100.

12-21   First we need to take a table of random numbers with a known variance. We would then draw many samples of 5 scores each. For each sample we would calculate the sample variance. When we had obtained several thousand sample variances, we would plot their frequency distribution. The fact that you are exceedingly unlikely to ever do this does not detract from the fact that you could do so. This is the clearest way to think about a sampling distribution.

Chapter 13 - Related-Samples *t* Test

==

13-1   Self-care skills taught through imitation and physical guidance:

We first need to calculate difference scores and then the mean and standard deviation of these difference scores. We can then solve for *t* using the standard formula.

Subject	Diff.
2	-2
3	4
4	3
5	1
6	3
7	5
8	-4
9	-2
10	7
11	5
12	-1
13	0
14	5
15	0

$$\overline{D} = \frac{\Sigma D}{N} = \frac{28}{15} = 1.87$$

$$s = \sqrt{\frac{200 - \dfrac{28^2}{15}}{14}} = 3.25$$

$$t = \frac{\overline{D} - 0}{\dfrac{s_D}{\sqrt{N}}} = \frac{1.87}{\dfrac{3.25}{\sqrt{15}}} = 2.226 \quad [t_{.025}(14) = \pm 2.145]$$

Reject H_0 because our calculated value of *t* (2.23) is larger than the critical value of *t* (±2.145), and conclude that physical guidance has reduced the amount of assistance required.

13-2   No, the answer is not clear, because the physical guidance condition always followed the imitation condition. Improvement may reflect just the passage of time or the delayed effects of imitation. Experiments in which the order of treatments is always the same confound treatment with time, and the results are ambiguous.

13-4   Confidence limits for the data in Exercise 13-1:

We know the mean and standard deviation from Exercise 13-1, and found the critical value of *t* there as well. We can calculate the standard error of the mean of differences as $s_D/\sqrt{N} = 3.25/\sqrt{15} = 0.84$. Now we simply have to substitute in the formula to find values that are t-standard errors above and below the mean.

$$CI_{.95} = \overline{D} \pm t_{.025}(s_{\overline{D}})$$

$$= 1.87 \pm (2.145)(0.84)$$

$$= 1.87 \pm 1.80$$

$$.07 \leq \mu_D \leq 3.67$$

An interval created in this way has a probability of 0.95 of enclosing the true population mean.

13-5   Effectiveness of advertising campaign to reduce smoking:

Again we calculate difference scores and their mean and standard deviation. We then solve for t.

Subject Diff.

Subject	Diff.
1	2
2	-4
3	3
4	3
5	5
6	0
7	-1
8	-3
9	3
10	-1
11	2
12	-4
13	-1
14	3
15	-2

$$\overline{D} = \frac{\Sigma D}{N} = \frac{5}{15} = 0.33$$

$$s_D = \sqrt{\frac{117 - \dfrac{5^2}{15}}{14}} = 2.87$$

$$t = \frac{\overline{D} - 0}{\dfrac{s_D}{\sqrt{N}}} = \frac{0.33}{\dfrac{2.87}{\sqrt{15}}} = 0.45$$

$$t_{.025}(14) = 2.145$$

Do not reject H_0. Our obtained value of t is far less than the critical value, meaning that a sample mean difference as large as this would occur quite frequently when the null hypothesis is true.

13-7   The data in Exercise 13-5 show that the program was not successful and had little effect on smokers. The data in Exercise 13-6 show larger effects. However, the program seems to have been successful for some subjects and to have led other subjects to smoke even more. These two results have canceled each other out and led to a nonsignificant t. The next step would be to examine the two groups differentiated in Exercise 13-6 to see how they differed. Did the program decrease smoking in women and increase it in men?   Were there differences between short-term and long--term smokers? And so on.

13-9   Are English grades higher than overall GPA in the Data Set?

Here we need to calculate the difference scores and then their mean and standard deviation.

Subject	ENGG	GPA	Diff.
1	3	2.60	0.40
2	3	2.75	0.25
3	4	4.00	0.00
4	2	2.25	-0.25
5	3	3.00	0.00
6	2	1.67	0.33
7	2	2.25	-0.25
8	4	3.40	0.60
9	1	1.33	-0.33
10	4	3.50	0.50
11	4	3.75	0.25
12	3	2.67	0.33
13	3	2.75	0.25
14	2	2.00	0.00
15	3	2.75	0.25
16	2	2.50	-0.50
17	4	3.55	0.45
18	3	2.75	0.25
19	4	3.50	0.50
20	2	2.75	-0.75

$$\overline{D} = \frac{2.28}{20} = 0.114$$

$$s_D = \sqrt{\frac{2.7992 - \frac{(2.28)^2}{20}}{19}} = 0.366$$

$$t = \frac{\overline{D} - 0}{\frac{s_D}{\sqrt{N}}} = \frac{0.114}{\frac{0.366}{\sqrt{20}}} = 1.39$$

$[t_{.025}(19) = \pm 2.09]$ Do not reject H_0

We have 19 degrees of freedom for this test because we have 20 pairs of observations. Note that it is the number of pairs and not the number of scores. Since our obtained t (1.39) is less than the critical value of t (± 2.09), we do not reject H_0.

13-10   From Exercise 13-5:

To answer this we need to know the critical value of t, which in turn requires knowing the *df*, which requires knowing N, which is what we're trying to calculate. But as a rough approximation, we can use 2.00 as a critical value. Then all that we need to do is to substitute the t that we seek (2.00) into the equation and solve for N.

$$t = \frac{\overline{D} - 0}{s_D / \sqrt{N}}$$

$$2.00 = \frac{0.333}{2.87 / \sqrt{N}}$$

$$N = 297.12$$

Therefore, 298 subjects would be needed to obtain a significant t.

13-12   As the correlation between the two variables increases, the t will increase as well. This is so because as the correlation increases, the standard deviation of the difference scores, and hence the standard error of the mean of difference scores, will decrease, giving a larger t.

Chapter 14 - t for Two Independent Samples

==

14-1 Imitation versus physical guidance in learning self-help skills, with different subjects in each group:

$$\overline{X}_1 = \frac{147}{15} = 9.8 \qquad\qquad \overline{X}_2 = \frac{103}{15} = 6.87$$

$$s_1^2 = \frac{1921 - \dfrac{(147)^2}{15}}{14} \qquad\qquad s_2^2 = \frac{1093 - \dfrac{(103)^2}{15}}{14}$$

$$= 34.31 \qquad\qquad\qquad = 27.55$$

$$t = \frac{\overline{X}_1 - \overline{X}_2}{\sqrt{\dfrac{s_1^2}{N_1} + \dfrac{s_2^2}{N_2}}} = \frac{9.8 - 6.87}{\sqrt{\dfrac{34.31}{15} + \dfrac{27.55}{15}}}$$

$$= 1.44$$

$$[t_{.025} = (28) = \pm 2.048]$$

Do not reject H_0 because the obtained value of t is below the critical value of t. We have 28 degrees of freedom here because we have two groups of 15 observations each. Therefore, we have 14 df in each group.

14-2 A significant difference was not found in Exercise 14-1 because of the large amounts of variability in each group. There is so much subject-to-subject variability that any difference that does exist between groups does not stand out sufficiently.

14-3 By measuring the same subject under both conditions in Exercise 13-1, we were able to eliminate the effects of subject-to-subject variability from the test. We only looked at the variability in the amount of *change* that people showed, not in their overall level of performance.

14-4   Effectiveness of reinforcement for feeding pets:

Here we need the mean and variance for each group, and then we only have to solve the equation for t.

$$\overline{X}_1 = \frac{21}{9} = 2.33 \qquad\qquad \overline{X}_2 = \frac{13}{9} = 1.44$$

$$s_1^2 = \frac{61 - \frac{(21)^2}{9}}{8} \qquad\qquad s_2^2 = \frac{29 - \frac{(13)^2}{9}}{8}$$

$$= 1.50 \qquad\qquad\qquad = 1.28$$

$$t = \frac{\overline{X}_1 - \overline{X}_2}{\sqrt{\frac{s_1^2}{N_1} + \frac{s_2^2}{N_2}}} = \frac{2.33 - 1.44}{\sqrt{\frac{1.50}{9} + \frac{1.28}{9}}}$$

$$= 1.601$$

$$[t_{.025}(16) = \pm 2.120]$$

Do not reject H_0 because the obtained value of t is less than the critical value. The *df* for this example = 16 because we have $n_i - 1 = 8$ *df* for each group.

14-6   Effectiveness of weightloss in program A versus weightloss in program B:

Here we have unequal sample sizes, so we must consider whether or not to pool the variances. Since the variances are nearly equal, it makes sense to pool them to get a better estimate of the common population variance of which they are both estimates.

$$\overline{X}_1 = \frac{136}{6} = 22.67 \qquad\qquad \overline{X}_2 = \frac{159}{12} = 13.25$$

$$s_1^2 = \frac{3174 - \dfrac{(136)^2}{6}}{5} \qquad\qquad s_2^2 = \frac{2291 - \dfrac{(159)^2}{12}}{11}$$

$$= 18.267 \qquad\qquad\qquad = 16.75$$

$$s_P^2 = \frac{(N_1 - 1)s_1^2 + (N_2 - 1)s_2^2}{N_1 - 1 + N_2 - 1}$$

$$= \frac{5(18.267) + 11(16.75)}{5 + 11} = 17.22$$

$$t = \frac{\overline{X}_1 - \overline{X}_2}{\sqrt{\dfrac{s_P^2}{N_1} + \dfrac{s_P^2}{N_2}}} = \frac{22.67 - 13.25}{\sqrt{\dfrac{17.22}{6} + \dfrac{17.22}{12}}}$$

$$= 4.54$$

$$[t_{.025}(16) = \pm 2.120]$$

We have $5 + 11 = 16$ degrees of freedom and can reject H_0 because the obtained value of t exceeds the critical value.

14-8 The differential dropout rate may be very important. Only half as many people were able to complete Program A as completed Program B. The program seems to work well for those who stayed in, but that does not necessarily make it a better program.

14-9 Studying the "experimenter bias" effect:

If there really is an experimenter bias effect in our study, we would expect the group means to differ because of the different instructions given to the groups.

$$\overline{X}_1 = \frac{169}{9} = 18.778 \qquad \overline{X}_2 = \frac{141}{8} = 17.625$$

$$s_1^2 = \frac{3297 - \frac{(169)^2}{9}}{8} \qquad s_2^2 = \frac{2607 - \frac{(141)^2}{8}}{7}$$

$$= 15.44 \qquad\qquad = 17.41$$

$$s_p^2 = \frac{(N_1 - 1)s_1^2 + (N_2 - 1)s_2^2}{N_1 - 1 + N_2 - 1}$$

$$= \frac{8(15.44) + 7(17.41)}{8 + 7} = 16.359$$

$$t = \frac{\overline{X}_1 - \overline{X}_2}{\sqrt{\frac{s_p^2}{N_1} + \frac{s_p^2}{N_2}}} = \frac{18.778 - 17.625}{\sqrt{\frac{16.359}{9} + \frac{16.359}{8}}}$$

$$= 0.587$$

$$[t_{.025}(15) = \pm 2.131]$$

We will not reject the null hypothesis because our obtained t is less than the critical value of t. I would conclude that there is no difference in performance as a function of the information given the experimenters.

14-10   Confidence limits for the data in Exercise 14-9:

The statistics we need are available from Exercise 14-9. We just need to calculate how large 2.131 standard errors is, and add and subtract that to and from the difference between the means. We want ±2.131 standard errors because the t distribution tells us that 95% of the observations will fall within that distance of the mean.

$$CI_{.95} = (\overline{X}_1 - \overline{X}_2) \pm t_{.025}\sqrt{\frac{s_p^2}{N_1} + \frac{s_p^2}{N_2}}$$

$$= (18.778 - 17.625) \pm 2.131\sqrt{\frac{16.359}{9} + \frac{16.359}{8}}$$

$$= 1.153 \pm 4.187$$

$$-3.034 \le (\mu_1 - \mu_2) \le 5.34$$

14-13 GPAs compared for ADDSC ≤ 65 versus ADDSC ≥ 66:

	ADDSC < 65	ADDSC > 66
$\overline{X} =$	194.30/75 = 2.59	21.85/13 = 1.68 [from Data Set]
$N =$	75	13
$s^2 =$	0.658	0.56

$$s_p^2 = \frac{(N_1 - 1)s_1^2 + (N_2 - 1)s_2^2}{N_1 + N_2 - 2}$$

$$= \frac{74(0.658) + 12(0.56)}{86} = 0.6443$$

$$t = \frac{\overline{X}_1 - \overline{X}_2}{\sqrt{\frac{s_p^2}{N_1} + \frac{s_p^2}{N_2}}} = \frac{2.59 - 1.68}{\sqrt{\frac{0.6443}{75} + \frac{0.6443}{13}}} = 3.76$$

$$[t_{.025}(86) = \pm 1.984]$$

We can reject H_0 because our obtained value of t is larger than the critical value. Students who had high ADDSC scores in elementary school had significantly lower grade point averages in 9th grade than did those who had lower scores.

14-14 ADDSC in elementary school is quite a good predictor of GPA in 9th grade. This is in fact somewhat worrisome, because it suggests long-term negative effects of early behavior patterns.

14-15 Innate ability versus time-filling tasks; dependent variable = number of problems solved:

If the instructions to subjects make a difference, and there is considerable reason to think they would from the psychological literature, then we would expect to find significant differences between the group means. Because sample sizes are equal, we do not need to worry about pooling variances, regardless of their values.

$$\overline{X}_1 = 27/5 = 5.4 \qquad N_1 = 5 \qquad s_1^2 = \frac{163 - \dfrac{(27)^2}{5}}{4} = 4.3$$

$$\overline{X}_2 = 42/5 = 8.4 \qquad N_1 = 5 \qquad s_2^2 = \frac{368 - \dfrac{(42)^2}{5}}{4} = 3.8$$

$$t = \frac{\overline{X}_1 - \overline{X}_2}{\sqrt{\dfrac{s_1^2}{N_1} + \dfrac{s_2^2}{N_2}}} = \frac{5.4 - 8.4}{\sqrt{\dfrac{4.3}{5} + \dfrac{3.8}{5}}} = -2.36$$

$[t_{.025}(8) = \pm 2.306]$

We will reject the null hypothesis because the obtained value of t (–2.36) is greater than the critical value. Notice that here "greater" means "more negative."

14-17 Pooled variance estimate with equal sample sizes:

A weighted average is the sum of each variance times its degrees of freedom, and then that sum divided by the total degrees of freedom.

$$s_p^2 = \frac{(N_1 - 1)s_1^2 + (N_2 - 1)s_2^2}{N_1 + N_2 - 2}$$

Because $N_1 = N_2$, we can replace them with the common symbol "N."

$$s_p^2 = \frac{(N_1 - 1)s_1^2 + (N_2 - 1)s_2^2}{N_1 + N_2 - 2}$$

$$= \frac{(N - 1)(s_1^2 + s_2^2)}{2(N - 1)}$$

$$= \frac{s_1^2 + s_2^2}{2}$$

With equal sample sizes, the pooled variance is equal to the arithmetic mean of the two sample variances.

14-19   A comparison of Exercises 14-15 and 14-16 shows that perfectly legitimate and reasonable transformations of data can produce different results. There is no rule to tell us which of these measures is "better" in some sense, and two different experimenters could quite easily use two different measures. The point is that it is important to consider seriously the nature of the dependent variable before beginning an experiment.

Chapter 15 - Power

==================

15-1   Mean SAT for entering freshmen at small N.E. college:

To calculate the power of this test we first need to estimate the effect size, then convert that to δ, and then use the tables to obtain the power of the test.

> **(a)** The effect size is the difference between the means divided by the standard deviation.

$$\gamma = \frac{\mu_1 - \mu_2}{\sigma} = \frac{520 - 500}{80} = 0.25$$

> **(b)** $f(N)$ for 1-sample t test $= \sqrt{N}$

$$\delta = \gamma / \sqrt{N} - 0.25\sqrt{100} = 2.5$$

> **(c)** power = .71   Therefore, the probability that this experiment will produce a result that is statistically significant is .71.

15-3   Changing power in Exercise 15-1:

To solve this problem we calculate the effect size and then look up the values of δ that correspond to the different levels of power. We then insert δ into the equation and solve for N. We have already found $\gamma = 0.25$.

> **(a)** For power = .70, $\delta = 2.475$

$$\delta = \gamma\sqrt{N}$$

$$2.475 = 0.25\sqrt{N}$$

$$N = 98.01 \approx 98$$

(b) For power = .80, $\delta = 2.8$

$$\delta = \gamma\sqrt{N}$$

$$2.8 = 0.25\sqrt{N}$$

$$N = 125.44 \approx 126$$

(c) For power = .90, $\delta = 3.25$

$$\delta = \gamma\sqrt{N}$$

$$3.25 = 0.25\sqrt{N}$$

$$N = 169$$

15-4   The N.E. college hopes for a 30-point gain in mean SAT:

Here we don't even need to know the values of μ. We are given the mean difference to begin with, and the standard deviation comes from Exercise 15-1.

$$\gamma = \frac{30}{80} = 0.375$$

$$\delta = 0.375\sqrt{100} = 3.75$$

power = .965

15-6   Avoidance behavior in rabbits using one-sample t test:

We can calculate the effect size from the information given. We can also obtain δ for power = .50 from the appendix. Then we just solve for N.

(a)

$$\gamma = \frac{\mu_1 - \mu_0}{\sigma} = \frac{5.8 - 4.8}{2} = 0.5$$

For power = .50, $\delta = 1.95$

$$\delta = \gamma\sqrt{N}$$

$$1.95 = 0.5\sqrt{N}$$

$$N = 15.21 \approx 16$$

(b) For power = .80, $\delta = 2.8$

$$\delta = \gamma\sqrt{N}$$

$$2.8 = 0.5\sqrt{N}$$

$$N = 31.36 \approx 32$$

15-8   Avoidance behavior in rabbits with unequal Ns:

From Exercise 15-6 we know the effect size. We then calculate the harmonic mean of the sample sizes and use that to solve for δ, and then for power.

$$\gamma = 0.5$$

$$N = \overline{N}_h = \frac{2N_1N_2}{N_1 + N_2}$$

$$= \frac{2(20)(15)}{20 + 15} = 17.14$$

$$\delta = \gamma\sqrt{N/2} = 0.5\sqrt{17.14/2}$$
$$= 1.46$$

power $= .31$

15-10   Modified data for Exercise 15-9:

In this problem we just repeat the earlier calculations with the new values.

(a) Power calculations:

$$\gamma = \frac{\mu_1 - \mu_0}{\sigma} = \frac{25 - 28}{8} = -0.375$$

$$\delta = \gamma\sqrt{N/2} = -0.375\sqrt{20/2}$$
$$= -1.19$$

power $= .22$

(b) t test:

$$t = \frac{\overline{X}_1 - \overline{X}_2}{\sqrt{\dfrac{s_p^2}{N_1} + \dfrac{s_p^2}{N_1}}}$$

$$= \frac{25 - 28}{\sqrt{\dfrac{64}{20} + \dfrac{64}{20}}} = -1.19$$

$[t_{.025}(38) = \pm 2.025]$

Do not reject H_0

(c) t is numerically equal to δ, although t is calculated from statistics and δ is calculated from parameters. In other words, $\delta =$ the t that you would get if the data came out the way you think the parameters are.

15-11 The significant t with the smaller N is the more impressive, for that test had less power, so the difference must have been larger to be significant.

15-14 Social awareness of ex-delinquents—which subject pool would be better to use?

The way to solve the student's dilemma is to calculate power for the two possible approaches and then to choose the approach with the greater power, which means with the greater value for δ.

$$\bar{X}_{normal} \quad -38 \qquad N = 50$$

$$\bar{X}_{college} \quad = 35 \qquad N = 100$$

$$\bar{X}_{dropout} \quad = 30 \qquad N = 25$$

$$\gamma = \frac{38 - 35}{\sigma} \qquad\qquad \gamma = \frac{38 - 30}{\sigma}$$

$$\overline{N}_h = \frac{2(50)(100)}{150} = 66.67 \qquad \overline{N}_h = \frac{2(50)(25)}{75} = 33.33$$

$$\delta = \frac{3}{\sigma}\sqrt{\frac{66.67}{2}} = \frac{17.32}{\sigma} \qquad \delta = \frac{8}{\sigma}\sqrt{\frac{33.33}{2}} = \frac{32.66}{\sigma}$$

Assuming equal standard deviations, the high school dropout group of 25 would result in a higher value of δ and therefore higher power than the delinquent group.

15-15 Total sample sizes required for power = .80, $\alpha = .01$, two-tailed (δ = 3.4):

Effect Size	γ	One-sample t	Two-sample t	
			Per Group	Overall
Small	.20	289	578	1156
Medium	.50	47	93	186
Large	.80	19	37	74

15-17 Can power ever be less than α?

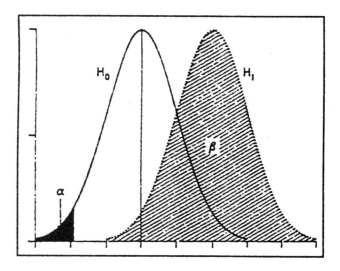

The preceding figure shows that power cannot be less than alpha unless we choose the wrong tail for our one-tailed test. In that case, power could be approximately zero.

15-18 When can power = β?

See the following figure. In that figure the mean under H_1 should fall at the critical value under H_0. The question implies a one-tailed test. Thus the mean is 1.645 standard errors above μ_0 which is 100.

$$\mu = 100 + 1.645\sigma_X$$

$$= 100 + 1.645(15/\sqrt{25})$$

$$= 104.935$$

When $\mu = 104.935$, power would equal β.

When Can Power = Beta?

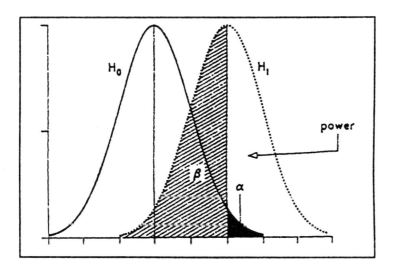

Chapter 16 - Oneway ANOVA
========================

16-1 Retrieval of rat pups:

First calculate the group totals, the Grand Total, and write out the sample sizes. Then solve the equations for the SS by substituting the relevant values.

$T_1 = 103$

$T_2 = 133$

$T_3 = 253$

$G = 489$

$N = 18$

$n = 6$

$$SS_{total} = \Sigma X^2 - \frac{G^2}{N}$$

$$= 15777 - \frac{(489)^2}{18} = 2492.5$$

$$SS_{group} = \frac{\Sigma T^2}{n} - \frac{G^2}{N}$$

$$= \frac{103^2 + 133^2 + 253^2}{6} - \frac{(489)^2}{18}$$

$$= 2100$$

$$SS_{error} = SS_{total} - SS_{group}$$

$$= 2492.5 - 2100 = 392.5$$

Source	df	SS	MS	F
Group (Age of Pup)	2	2100.0	1050.000	40.127*
Error	15	392.5	26.167	
Total	17	2492.5		

*$p < .05$ [$F_{.05}(2,15) = 3.68$]

Because F_{obt} is greater than the critical value of F, we can reject H_0 and conclude that the retrieval rate for pups varies with their ages. Moms become more tolerant as the kids grow up.

16-2   Protected t tests on the data in Exercise 16-1:

Because the overall F in Exercise 16-1 was significant, we can go ahead and compare the groups using standard t tests, substituting MS_{error} for the variance terms.

5 – versus 20 – day – old pups :   20 – versus 35 – day – old pups :

$\overline{X}_1 = 17.167$ $\overline{X}_2 = 22.167$ $\overline{X}_3 = 42.167$

$$t = \frac{\overline{X}_2 - \overline{X}_1}{\sqrt{\dfrac{MS_{error}}{n} + \dfrac{MS_{error}}{n}}} \qquad t = \frac{\overline{X}_3 - \overline{X}_2}{\sqrt{\dfrac{MS_{error}}{n} + \dfrac{MS_{error}}{n}}}$$

$$= \frac{22.167 - 17.167}{\sqrt{\dfrac{26.167}{6} + \dfrac{26.167}{6}}} \qquad = \frac{42.167 - 22.167}{\sqrt{\dfrac{26.167}{6} + \dfrac{26.167}{6}}}$$

$= 1.69$ $= 6.773$

Do not reject H_0 Reject H_0

$$[t_{.025}(15) = \pm 2.131]$$

We would conclude that there is not a significant difference between the retrieval times for the two youngest groups of pups, but there is a significantly longer retrieval time for the 35-day-old pups.

16-4   Effects of brand and location of cigarettes on consumer buying behavior:

This is just an extension of the previous problems to the case of four groups. The calculations are the same.

(a) ANOVA:

$T_1 = 143$

$T_2 = 146$

$T_3 = 64$

$T_4 = 99$

$G = 452$

$N = 28$

$n = 7$

$$SS_{total} = \Sigma X^2 - \frac{G^2}{N}$$

$$= 8438 - \frac{(452)^2}{28} = 1141.4286$$

$$SS_{group} = \frac{\Sigma T^2}{n} - \frac{G^2}{N}$$

$$= \frac{143^2 + 146^2 + 64^2 + 99^2}{7} - \frac{(452)^2}{28}$$

$$= 655.1429$$

$$SS_{error} = SS_{total} - SS_{group}$$

$$= 1141.4286 - 655.1429 = 486.2857$$

Source	df	SS	MS	F
Group	3	655.1429	218.3810	10.778*
Error	24	486.2857	20.2619	
Total	27	1141.4286		

*$p < .05$ [$F_{.05}(3,24) = 3.01$]

(b) ANOVA on groups 1 + 3 versus 2 + 4:

Here we just lump together the observations in Groups 1 and 3 and treat them as one large group. We do the same for Groups 2 and 4.

$T_{1+3} = 207$ SS_{total} = Same as above = 1141.4286

$T_{2+4} = 245$

$$SS_{group} = \frac{\Sigma T^2}{n} - \frac{G^2}{N}$$

$$= \frac{207^2 + 245^2}{14} - \frac{(452)^2}{18}$$

$$= 51.5714$$

$$SS_{error} = SS_{total} - SS_{group}$$

$$= 1141.4286 - 51.5714 = 1089.8572$$

Source	df	SS	MS	F
Group	1	51.5714	51.5714	1.230 ns
Error	26	1089.8572	41.9176	
Total	27	1141.4286		

$[F_{.05}(1,26) = 4.23]$

This F tests the null hypothesis that the display of a product in a prominent place is no different from the display in the usual place, disregarding the popularity of the brands. Because F is less than the critical value of F, we cannot conclude that the location makes a difference.

16-6 Modification of Exercise 16-3 (cost of entrées) to have unequal Ns:

The purpose of this is to illustrate an analysis of variance with unequal sample sizes and to illustrate that the analysis of variance pools group variances.

(a) ANOVA:

$T_1 = 67.50$

$n_1 = \quad 7$ $\qquad SS_{total} = \Sigma X^2 - \dfrac{G^2}{N}$

$T_2 = 51.50$ $\qquad\qquad = 1195.875 - \dfrac{(119)^2}{12} = 15.792$

$n_2 = \quad 5$

$G = \quad 119$ $\qquad SS_{group} = \dfrac{\Sigma T^2}{n} - \dfrac{G^2}{N}$

$N = \quad 12$

$$= \dfrac{67.50^2}{7} + \dfrac{51.50^2}{5} - \dfrac{(119)^2}{12}$$

$$= 1.260$$

$$SS_{error} = SS_{total} - SS_{group}$$

$$= 15.792 - 1.260 = 14.532$$

Source	df	SS	MS	F
Group (Host/Guest)	1	1.260	1.260	.867 ns
Error	10	14.532	1.453	
Total	11	15.792		

$[F_{.05}(1,10) = 4.96]$

(b) Independent t test without pooling:

$\bar{X}_1 = 9.643$

$s_1{}^2 = 1.102$

$n_1 = 7$

$\bar{X}_2 = 10.30$

$s_2{}^2 = 1.98$

$n_2 = 5$

$$t = \frac{\bar{X}_1 - \bar{X}_2}{\sqrt{\dfrac{s_1^2}{n_1} + \dfrac{s_2^2}{n_2}}}$$

$$= \frac{9.643 - 10.300}{\sqrt{\dfrac{1.102}{7} + \dfrac{1.98}{5}}}$$

$$= -0.883$$

$[t_{.025}(10) = \pm 2.228]$

Do not reject H_0.

(c) Independent t test pooling variance:

$$s_p^2 = \frac{(n_1 - 1)s_1^2 + (n_2 - 1)s_2^2}{n_1 + n_2 - 2}$$

$$= \frac{(7 - 1)(1.102) + (5 - 1)(1.98)}{7 + 5 - 2} = 1.4532$$

$$t = \frac{\bar{X}_1 - \bar{X}_2}{\sqrt{\dfrac{s_p^2}{n_1} + \dfrac{s_p^2}{n_2}}}$$

$$= \frac{9.643 - 10.300}{\sqrt{\dfrac{1.4532}{7} + \dfrac{1.4532}{5}}}$$

$$= -0.931$$

$t_{.025}(10) = \pm 2.228]$ Do not reject H_0.

(d) $t(\text{pooled})^2 = (-.931)^2 = .867 = F$

Notice also that the pooled variance estimate is exactly equal to MS_{error} in the analysis of variance.

16-7   Magnitude of effect for data in Exercise 16-3:

This is a simple matter of substituting information from Exercise 16-3.

$$\eta^2 = \frac{SS_{group}}{SS_{total}}$$

$$= \frac{2.2562}{11.5062} = 0.196$$

$$\omega^2 = \frac{SS_{group} - (k-1)MS_{error}}{SS_{total} + MS_{error}}$$

$$= \frac{2.2562 - (2-1)1.1562}{11.5062 + 1.1562} = 0.087$$

16-8   Effect of capitalization of words in a prose passage:

(a) ANOVA:

$T_1 = 302$ $s_1^2 = 38.5641$ $G = 941$

$T_2 = 383$ $s_2^2 = 57.0025$ $N = 30$

$T_3 = 256$ $s_3^2 = 33.0625$ $n = 10$

$$SS_{group} = \frac{\Sigma T^2}{n} - \frac{G^2}{N}$$

$$= \frac{302^2 + 383^2 + 256^2}{10} - \frac{(941)^2}{30}$$

$$= 826.8667$$

$$MS_{error} = \overline{s}^2 = \frac{38.5641 + 57.0025 + 33.0625}{3}$$

$$= 42.8764$$

Source	df	SS	MS	F
Group	2	826.8667	413.4334	9.642*
Error	27	1157.6628	42.8764	
Total	29	1984.5295		

*$p < .05$ $[F_{.05}(2,27) = 3.355]$

Capitalizing none of the words, a random set of words, or the important words in a prose passage has an effect on its readability as measured by the time taken to read it.

(b) It does not compare good and poor readers—nor do we even know how well any of our subjects read.

(c) Capitalization influences reading speed.

16-10   Protected t tests on data in Exercise 16-8:

Group 1 versus Group 2:   Group 1 versus Group 3:

$$\overline{X}_1 = 30.2 \qquad \overline{X}_2 = 38.3 \qquad \overline{X}_3 = 25.6$$

$$t = \frac{\overline{X}_2 - \overline{X}_1}{\sqrt{\dfrac{MS_{error}}{n} + \dfrac{MS_{error}}{n}}} \qquad\qquad t = \frac{\overline{X}_3 - \overline{X}_1}{\sqrt{\dfrac{MS_{error}}{n} + \dfrac{MS_{error}}{n}}}$$

$$= \frac{38.3 - 30.2}{\sqrt{\dfrac{42.876}{6} + \dfrac{42.876}{6}}} \qquad\qquad = \frac{25.6 - 30.2}{\sqrt{\dfrac{42.876}{6} + \dfrac{42.876}{6}}}$$

$$= 2.766 \qquad\qquad\qquad\qquad = -1.57$$

Reject H_0 Do not reject H_0

$$[t_{.025}(15) = \pm 2.131]$$

Capitalizing a random set of words significantly slows down reading, but capitalizing the important words does not significantly speed it up. (Notice that we have 15 df for the t test because the MS_{error} in the Anova had 15 df.

16-11 I have somewhat more faith in the significant F in Exercise 16-9 than in Exercise 16-10 because it is a significant result produced by a less powerful experiment.

16-14 ANOVA on GPAs for three levels of ADDSC:

(1) ADDSC < 40	(2) ADDSC = 41 – 59	(3) ADDSC > 60	
$n = 14$	$n = 49$	$n = 25$	$N = 88$
$\Sigma X = 45.55$	$\Sigma X = 127.01$	$\Sigma X = 43.59$	$G = 216.15$

$$SS_{total} = \Sigma X^2 - \frac{G^2}{N}$$

$$= 595.477 - \frac{(216.15)^2}{88} = 64.559$$

$$SS_{group} = \frac{\Sigma T^2}{n} - \frac{G^2}{N}$$

$$= \frac{45.55^2}{49} + \frac{127.01^2}{49} + \frac{43.59^2}{25} - \frac{(216.15)^2}{188}$$

$$= 22.500$$

$$SS_{error} = SS_{total} - SS_{group}$$

$$= 64.559 - 22.500 = 42.059$$

Source	df	SS	MS	F
Group (ADDSC level)	2	22.500	11.250	22.74*
Error	85	42.059	.495	
Total	87	64.559		

$*p < .05 \quad [F_{.05}(2,85) = 3.11]$

16-15   Magnitude of effect for Exercise 16-14:

$$\eta^2 = \frac{SS_{group}}{SS_{total}}$$

$$= \frac{22.500}{64.559} - 0.348$$

$$\omega^2 = \frac{SS_{group} - (k-1)MS_{error}}{SS_{total} + MS_{error}}$$

$$= \frac{22.500 - (3-1)0.459}{64.559 + 0.459} = 0.331$$

16-18   Scheffé's test for the data in Exercise 16-1:

5- versus 20-day-old pups: 20- versus 35-day-old pups:

$t = 1.69$ $t = 6.773$

$F = t^2 = 2.856$ $F = t^2 = 45.874$

Do not reject H_0.   Reject H_0.

Critical value for $F = (k-1)F_{(K-1),k(n-1)} = 2(3.68) = 7.36$

These are the same decisions we made in Exercise 16-2.

16.21   Analysis of Spilich's data on Pattern Recognition:

The Systat printout follows:

```
DEP VAR: LATENCY         N:      45  MULTIPLE R: 0.049
                                     SQUARED MULTIPLE R: 0.002


                       ANALYSIS OF VARIANCE

SOURCE      SUM-OF-SQUARES  DF MEAN-SQUARE    F-RATIO       P
GROUP$          2.17778      2     1.08889    0.05115  0.95020
ERROR         894.13333     42    21.28889

LEAST SQUARES MEANS.
                                 LS MEAN             SE      N
     GROUP$    =Active          9.40000        1.19133     15
     GROUP$    =Delayed         9.60000        1.19133     15
     GROUP$    =NonSmoker       9.93333        1.19133     15
```

The group means are plotted below:

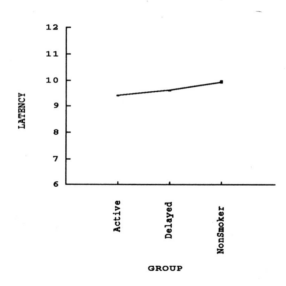

From this analysis we see that smoking status has no reliable effect on performance in a pattern recognition task.

16.24 Analysis of Driving Simulation task:

```
DEP VAR:COLLISIO        N:      45  MULTIPLE R: 0.553
                                    SQUARED MULTIPLE R: 0.306

                        ANALYSIS OF VARIANCE

SOURCE      SUM-OF-SQUARES  DF  MEAN-SQUARE   F-RATIO     P
GROUP$        437.64444     2    218.82222    9.25843  0.00047
ERROR         992.66667    42     23.63492


LEAST SQUARES MEANS
                                 LS MEAN          SE        N
       GROUP$   =Active         9.93333     1.25525       15
       GROUP$   =Delayed        6.80000     1.25525       15
       GROUP$   =NonSmoker      2.33333     1.25525       15
```

In this analysis there are significant differences among the three groups ($p -$ .0005). By visual inspection it appears that Active smokers perform very much worse than the other two groups, who show only minor differences between them. (The Delayed and NonSmoker groups would not differ by a Bonferroni test—or even by Fisher's LSD test.)

16-25 The three different experiments by Spilich et al. (1992) involved different levels of cognitive processing. In the task with the fewest requirements, there were no differences among the groups. In a task requiring the comprehension of a written passage, nonsmokers significantly outperformed smokers, who did not differ between the Active and Delayed groups. The driving simulation task required a different kind of cognitive processing, and in that task the active smokers differed from the other two groups, who did not differ from each other.

Chapter 17 - Factorial ANOVA
===============================

17-1   Factorial ANOVA (Sex versus Host/Guest) on price of entrées:

In this problem we have an additional independent variable that we did not have in Chapter 16. First we need the cell totals, which are shown below.

	Host	Guest	
Male	40.50	49.00	89.50
Female	44.00	44.25	88.25
	84.50	93.25	177.75 = G

$$\Sigma X^2 = 1592.9375 \quad N = 20 \quad n = 5 \quad s = 2 \quad h = 2$$

$$SS_{total} = \Sigma X^2 = \frac{G^2}{N} = 1592.9375 - \frac{177.75^2}{20} = 13.184$$

The sums of squares for Host and Sex are found just as in a one-way.

$$SS_H = \frac{\Sigma T_H^2}{sn} - \frac{G^2}{N}$$

$$= \frac{84.5^2 + 93.25^2}{2(5)} - \frac{177.75^2}{20} = 3.828$$

$$SS_S = \frac{\Sigma T_S^2}{hn} - \frac{G^2}{N}$$

$$= \frac{89.5^2 + 88.25^2}{2(5)} - \frac{177.75^2}{20} = 0.078$$

The interaction sums of squares are found from cell totals.

$$SS_{Cells} = \frac{\Sigma T^2_{Cell}}{n} - \frac{G^2}{N}$$

$$= \frac{40.5^2 + 49^2 + 44^2 + 44.25^2}{5} - \frac{177.75^2}{20} = 7.309$$

$SS_{HS} = SS_{cells} - SS_H - SS_S = 7.309 - 3.828 - .078 = 3.403$

$SS_{error} = SS_{total} - SS_{cells} = 13.184 - 7.309 = 5.875$

Source	df	SS	MS	F
Host/Guest	1	3.828	3.828	10.43*
Sex	1	0.078	0.078	< 1
H X S	1	3.403	3.403	9.27*
Error	16	5.875	0.367	
Total	19	13.184		

* $p < .05$ [$F_{.05}(1,16) = 4.49$]

We can conclude that there is a significant interaction between the sex of the couple and who is the host. (It would appear that there is quite a difference between Host and Guest for male couples, but not for female couples.) There is also a Host/Guest main effect, but interpretation is difficult because of the interaction.

17-2   Mother/infant interaction for primiparous/multiparous mothers with LBW or full-term infants:

The cell totals are shown below. The solution follows the same model as the one in Exercise 17-1.

		Weight		
		LBW	F-T	
Parity	Primi-	53	64	117
	Multi-	69	82	151
		122	146	268 = G

$$\Sigma X^2 = 2010 \quad N = 40 \quad n = 10 \quad w = 2 \quad p = 2$$

$$SS_{total} = \Sigma X^2 - \frac{G^2}{N} = 2010 - \frac{268^2}{40} = 214.4$$

$$SS_P = \frac{\Sigma T_P^2}{wn} - \frac{G^2}{N}$$

$$= \frac{117^2 + 151^2}{2(10)} - \frac{268^2}{40} = 28.9$$

$$SS_W = \frac{\Sigma T_W^2}{pn} - \frac{G^2}{N}$$

$$= \frac{122^2 + 146^2}{2(10)} - \frac{268^2}{40} = 14.4$$

$$SS_{cell} = \frac{\Sigma T_{cell}^2}{n} - \frac{G^2}{N}$$

$$= \frac{53^2 + 64^2 + 69^2 + 82^2}{10} - \frac{268^2}{40} = 43.4$$

$$SS_{PW} = SS_{cells} - SS_p - SS_W = 43.4 - 28.9 - 14.4 = 0.1$$

$$SS_{error} = SS_{total} - SS_{cells} = 214.4 - 43.4 = 171.0$$

Source	df	SS	MS	F
Parity	1	28.9	28.9	6.08 *
Weight	1	14.4	14.4	3.03ns
P x W	1	.1	.1	< 1
Error	36	171.0	4.75	
Total	39	214.4		

$*p < .05$ $[F_{.05}(1,36) = 4.12]$

There is a significant effect due to Parity, but not due to Weight or the Parity x Weight (P x W) interaction.

17-3   The mean for these primiparous mothers would not be expected to be a good estimate of the mean for the population of all primiparous mothers because 50% of our data points came from primiparous mothers, but 50% of the population of primiparous mothers do not give birth to LBW infants.

17-4   Simple effects of Weight for Multiparous mothers in Exercise 17-2:

To get the simple effects we need to analyze the data just for the specific subgrouping of interest. Thus we start off with just the data for the multiparous mothers.

		Weight		
		LBW	F-T	
Parity	Primi-	53	64	117
	Multi-	69	82	151
		122	146	268 = G

$$SS_{W \, at \, M} = \frac{\Sigma T^2_{W \, at \, M}}{n} - \frac{T^2_M}{wn} = \frac{69^2 + 82^2}{10} - \frac{151^2}{2(10)} = 8.45$$

$$MS_{W \, at \, M} = \frac{SS_{W \, at \, M}}{1} = 8.45$$

$$F_{W \, at \, M} = \frac{MS_{W \, at \, M}}{MS_{error}} = \frac{8.45}{4.75} = 1.78 \; ns$$

$[F_{.05}(1,36) = 4.12]$

17-7 Protected t test to compare Neutral Site to each of the others in Exercise 17-5:

We can use the protected t to compare Site means because the overall effect for site was significant. We would not use that test to compare Delay conditions, however, because Delay was not significant.

$$t = \frac{\overline{N} - \overline{A}}{\sqrt{\dfrac{MS_{error}}{n_N} + \dfrac{MS_{error}}{n_A}}} \qquad\qquad t = \frac{\overline{N} - \overline{B}}{\sqrt{\dfrac{MS_{error}}{n_N} + \dfrac{MS_{error}}{n_B}}}$$

$$= \frac{28.20 - 22.20}{\sqrt{\dfrac{29.311}{15} + \dfrac{29.311}{15}}} \qquad\qquad = \frac{28.20 - 22.27}{\sqrt{\dfrac{29.311}{15} + \dfrac{29.311}{15}}}$$

$$= 3.03 \;\; (\text{Reject } H_0) \qquad\qquad\qquad = 3.00 \;\; (\text{Reject } H_0)$$

$[t_{.025}(36) = \pm 2.03]$

We can conclude that both the difference between Groups N and A and between Groups N and B are significant.

17-10 Data in Exercise 16-4 (Brand and Location of cigarettes) analyzed as a factorial:

This problem is an extension of the one-way ANOVA in Exercise 16-4, designed to show the similarities and differences.

		Brand		
		Known	Unknown	
Location	Usual	143	64	207
	Prominent	146	99	245
		289	163	$452 = G$

$\Sigma X^2 = 8438 \quad N = 28 \quad n = 7 \quad l = 2 \quad b = 2$

$SS_{total} = 1141.43$ [same as Ex.164]

$$SS_B = \frac{\Sigma T_B^2}{ln} - \frac{G^2}{N}$$

$$= \frac{289^2 + 163^2}{2(7)} - \frac{452^2}{28} = 567.00$$

$$SS_L = \frac{\Sigma T_L^2}{bn} - \frac{G^2}{N}$$

$$= \frac{207^2 + 245^2}{2(7)} - \frac{452^2}{28} = 51.57$$

$$SS_{cells} = \frac{\Sigma T_{cell}^2}{n} - \frac{G^2}{N} = 655.14 \quad [= SS_{group} \text{ in EX } 16.4]$$

$$SS_{BL} = SS_{cells} - SS_B - SS_L = 655.14 - 567.00 - 51.57 = 36.57$$

$$SS_{error} = SS_{total} - SS_{cells} = 1141.43 - 655.14 = 486.29 \quad [\text{same as Ex} 16.4]$$

Source	df	SS	MS	F
Brand	1	567.00	567.00	27.99 *
Location	1	51.57	51.57	2.55 ns
B x L	1	36.57	36.57	1.81 ns
Error	24	486.29	20.26	
Total	27	1141.43		

$* p < .05$ $[F_{.05}(1,24) = 4.26]$

There is an effect for Brand, but not for Location or the Interaction. Notice that $SS_{Location}$ is the same in both analyses. The error term is smaller here, however, because we have also removed Brand differences and the Brand x Location (B x L)interaction from error. This gives more power.

17-11 The oneway ANOVA in Exercise 16-4(b) between Groups 1 and 3 versus 2 and 4 in comparison to the main effect of Location in the 2-way ANOVA in Exercise 17-10:

The SS_{group} is the same in both cases, but in the 2-way ANOVA, SS_B and SS_{BL} have been separated out of the SS_{error} leaving a smaller SS_{error}. This variation is left in SS_{error} in the oneway ANOVA.

17-18 Analysis of three experiments on smoking and performance:

(a)   We do not have any real interest in the effect of task itself because the dependent variable is measured in different units in the three tasks. However, by including it in the analysis we can look at the interaction, which is of interest.

(b)   The analysis of variance:

The following output came from Systat.

```
DEP VAR:   DEPVAR        N:       135  MULTIPLE R: 0.837
                                       SQUARED MULTIPLE R: 0.700

                         ANALYSIS OF VARIANCE

SOURCE       SUM-OF-SQUARES DF   MEAN-SQUARE    F-RATIO      P

SMOKGRP        354.548148    2    177.274074    1.643939  0.197334
TASK           .286615E+05   2    .143308E+05 132.895382  0.000000
SMOKGRP
*TASK         2728.651852    4    682.162963    6.325993  0.000113
ERROR          .135872E+05 126    107.834921
```

Note: The notation ".286615E+05" is called exponential notation and tells you to multiply .286615 * 10⁵. Just move the decimal point 5 places to the right to get 28661.5.

From this analysis we see that there is no significant effect for SmokGrp. There is an effect for Task, but, as noted, we are not interested in that effect. There is also a significant interaction that tells us that the effect of smoking varies with the task the subject is trying to do. This is the major effect of interest in this experiment.

   (c)   Plot of the means:

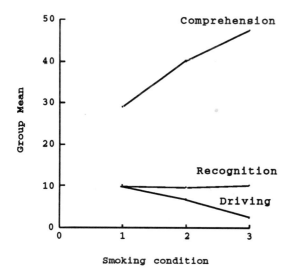

131

Chapter 18 - Repeated Measures ANOVA

===================================

18-1 Does taking the GRE repeatedly lead to higher scores?

The following table just gives the subject totals that you will need for the analysis. The rest of the data are in the question.

Test Session

Subject	1	2	3	Total	
1				1700	$N = 24$
2				1350	
3				1850	$s = 8$
4				1990	
5				1310	$t = 3$
6				2090	
7				1510	
8				1720	

$\Sigma X^2 = 7811200$

$$\quad\quad 4420 \quad 4510 \quad 4590 \quad 13520 = G$$

$$SS_{total} = \Sigma X^2 - \frac{G^2}{N}$$

$$= 7811200 - \frac{13520^2}{24} = 194933.33$$

$$SS_{Subj} = \frac{\Sigma T_s^2}{t} - \frac{G^2}{N}$$

$$= \frac{1700^2 + \cdots + 1720^2}{3} - \frac{13520^2}{24} = 189666.66$$

$$SS_{test} = \frac{\Sigma T_t^2}{s} - \frac{G^2}{N}$$

$$= \frac{4420^2 + 4510^2 + 4590^2}{8} - \frac{13520^2}{24} = 1808.33$$

$$SS_{error} = SS_{total} - SS_{Subj} - SS_{test}$$

$$= 194933.33 - 189666.66 - 1808.33 = 3458.37$$

Source	df	SS	MS	F
Subjects	7	189666.66		
Test Session	2	1808.33	904.17	3.66 ns
Error	14	3458.33	247.02	
Total	23	194933.33		

$$[F_{.05}(2,14) = 3.74]$$

Because the F value is not significant, we would have to conclude that we do not have sufficient data to reject the hypothesis that practice has no effect on GRE performance.

18-3   Teaching of self-care skills to severely retarded children: The following are the subject totals.

Subj	Base	Train	F-U	Total	
1				24	$\Sigma X^2 = 1100$
2				17	$N = 30$
3	data not shown			8	$s = 10$
4				14	
5				16	$t = 3$
6				22	
7				19	
8				18	
9				14	
10				18	
	$\overline{48}$	$\overline{70}$	$\overline{52}$	$\overline{170} = G$	

$$SS_{total} = \Sigma X^2 - \frac{G^2}{N}$$

$$= 1100 - \frac{170^2}{30} = 136.67$$

$$SS_{Subj} = \frac{\Sigma T_s^2}{t} - \frac{G^2}{N}$$

$$= \frac{24^2 + \cdots + 18^2}{3} - \frac{170^2}{30} = 60.00$$

$$SS_{test} = \frac{\Sigma T_t^2}{s} - \frac{G^2}{N}$$

$$= \frac{48^2 + 70^2 + 52^2}{10} - \frac{170^2}{30} = 27.47$$

$$SS_{error} = SS_{total} - SS_{Subj} - SS_{test}$$

$$= 136.67 - 60.00 - 27.47 = 49.20$$

Source	df	SS	MS	F
Subjects	9	60.00		
Test Session	2	27.47	13.735	5.03*
Error	18	49.20	2.733	
Total	29	136.67		

*$p < .05$ $[F_{.05}(2,18) = 3.55]$

Here we can reject the null hypothesis and conclude that the training experience makes a difference in performance. We still don't know the nature of that difference.

18-4 Protected t tests on data in Exercise 18-3:

Baseline versus Training:

$$t = \frac{\overline{B} - \overline{T}}{\sqrt{\dfrac{MS_{error}}{n_B} + \dfrac{MS_{error}}{n_T}}}$$

$$= \frac{4.8 - 7.0}{\sqrt{\dfrac{2.733}{10} + \dfrac{2.733}{10}}}$$

$$= -2.976 \quad (\text{Reject } H_0)$$

Baseline versus Follow-Up:

$$t = \frac{\overline{B} - \overline{F}}{\sqrt{\dfrac{MS_{error}}{n_B} + \dfrac{MS_{error}}{n_F}}}$$

$$= \frac{4.8 - 5.2}{\sqrt{\dfrac{2.733}{10} + \dfrac{2.733}{10}}}$$

$$= -0.541 \quad (\text{Do not reject } H_0)$$

$[t_{.025}(18) = \pm 2.101]$

Performance improved from Baseline to Training, but after training was discontinued the children were not significantly better in self-care skills than before training began.

18-10 Two baseline weeks in Table 18-1:

The point of this exercise is to demonstrate the similarities between the analysis of variance and t in this situation.

Subj	Base$_1$	Base$_2$	Total	Diff
1	21	22	43	1
2	20	19	39	-1
3	7	5	12	-2
4	25	30	55	5
5	30	33	63	3
6	19	27	46	8
7	26	16	42	-10
8	13	4	17	-9
9	26	24	50	-2
totals:	187	180	367	-7

(a) Repeated measures ANOVA:

$\sum X^2 = 8733 \quad N = 18 \quad s = 9 \quad w = 2$

$$SS_{total} = \Sigma X^2 - \frac{G^2}{N}$$

$$= 8733 - \frac{367^2}{18} = 1250.28$$

$$SS_{Subj} = \frac{\Sigma T_s^2}{w} - \frac{G^2}{N}$$

$$= \frac{43^2 + \cdots + 50^2}{2} - \frac{367^2}{18} = 1105.78$$

$$SS_{week} = \frac{\Sigma T_w^2}{s} - \frac{G^2}{N}$$

$$= \frac{187^2 + 180^2}{9} - \frac{367^2}{18} = 2.72$$

$$SS_{error} = SS_{total} - SS_{Subj} - SS_{test}$$

$$= 1250.28 - 1105.78 - 2.72 = 142.23$$

Source	df	SS	MS	F
Subjects	8	1105.78		
Week	1	2.72	2.72	0.153 ns
Error	8	142.23	17.78	
Total	17	136.67		

$[F_{.05}(1,8) = 5.32]$

(b) Related samples t test:

$$\overline{D} = \frac{-7}{9} = -0.777 \quad N = 9$$

$$s_D = \sqrt{\frac{\Sigma D^2 - \frac{(\Sigma D)^2}{N}}{N-1}} = \sqrt{\frac{289 - \frac{(-7)^2}{9}}{8}} = 5.95$$

$$t = \frac{\overline{D} - 0}{s_D / \sqrt{N}} = \frac{-0.777}{5.95 / \sqrt{9}} = 0.3915$$

$[t_{.025}(8) = \pm 2.306]$ Do not reject H_0.

(c) Comparison of F and t:

$$\sqrt{F} = \sqrt{0.153} = 0.391 = t$$

Notice that you get the same answer (except that $F = t^2$) whichever way you approach the problem.

Chapter 19 - Chi-Square
=========================

19-1   Popularity of Psychology professors:

For this problem we obtain the expected values by dividing the total sample size equally among the three instructors.

	Anderson	Klansky	Kamm	Total
Observed	25	32	10	67
Expected	22.3	22.3	22.3	67

$$\chi^2 = \sum \frac{(O - E)^2}{E}$$

$$= \frac{(25 - 22.3)^2}{22.3} + \frac{(32 - 22.3)^2}{22.3} + \frac{(10 - 22.3)^2}{22.3}$$

$$= 11.33$$

$$[\chi^2_{.05}(2) = 5.99]$$

Reject H_0 and conclude that students do not enroll at random.

19-2   We cannot tell in Exercise 19-1 if students chose different sessions because of the instructor or because of the times at which the sessions are taught—Instructor and Time are confounded. We would *at least* have to offer the sections at the same time.

19-3   Sorting one-sentence characteristics into piles:

Notice that these expected frequencies are not all equal to each other because our theory predicts that we would expect more observations in some categories than others.

	1	2	3	4	5	Total
Observed	8	10	20	8	4	50
Expected	5	10	20	10	5	50
Exp. %	10%	20%	40%	20%	10%	100%

$$\chi^2 = \sum \frac{(O - E)^2}{E}$$

$$= \frac{(8-5)^2}{5} + \frac{(10-10)^2}{10} + \frac{(20-20)^2}{20} + \frac{(8-10)^2}{10} + \frac{(4-5)^2}{5}$$

$$= 2.4$$

$[\chi^2 {}_{.05}(4) - 9.49]$

Do not reject H_0 that my daughter's sorting behavior is in line with my theory. I would have needed a $\chi^2 \geq 9.49$, and the one I obtained was only 2.4.

19-4   The answer in Exercise 19-3 generalizes only to the population of data that could be generated by my daughter. In other words, we have only a sample of *her* behavior. We do not have a random sample of the behavior of people in general, and therefore have trouble generalizing about them.

19-5   Racial choice in dolls (Clark & Clark, 1939):

In this test we only wish to see if the children chose a disproportionate number of dolls of one color.

	Black	White	Total
Observed	83	169	252
Expected	126	126	252

$$\chi^2 = \sum \frac{(O - E)^2}{E}$$

$$= \frac{(83 - 126)^2}{126} + \frac{(169 - 126)^2}{126}$$

$$= 29.35$$

$$[\chi^2_{.05}(1) = 3.84]$$

Reject H_0 and conclude that the children did not chose dolls at random (at least with respect to color). They chose white dolls predominately.

19-7 Combining the two racial-choice experiments:

This is an entirely different question. We want to know whether the pattern of choices has changed with time, presumably with the increase in racial awareness among black children. (Expected values are in parentheses.)

	Black	White	
1939	83	169	252
	(106.42)	(145.58)	
1970	61	28	89
	(37.58)	(51.42)	
	144	197	341

$$\chi^2 = \sum \frac{(O - E)^2}{E}$$

$$= \frac{(83 - 106.42)^2}{106.42} + \frac{(169 - 145.58)^2}{145.58}$$

$$+ \frac{(61 - 37.58)^2}{37.58} + \frac{(28 - 51.42)^2}{51.42}$$

$$= 34.184$$

$$[\chi^2_{.05}(1) = 3.84]$$

140

Reject H_0 and conclude that the distribution of choices between Black and White dolls was different in the two studies. Choice is *not* independent of Study. We are no longer asking whether one color of doll is preferred over the other color, but whether the *pattern* of preference is constant across studies. In analysis of variance terms we are dealing with an interaction.

19-10 Prediction of High School English level from ADD classification in elementary school:

The expected values are given in the table in parentheses below the obtained values (e.g., $E_{12} = 209*261/302$).

	Remedial	Regular	
Normal	22 (28.374)	187 (180.626)	209
ADD	19 (12.626)	74 (80.374)	93
	41	261	302

$$\chi^2 = \sum \frac{(O - E)^2}{E}$$

$$= \frac{(22 - 28.374)^2}{28.374} + \frac{(187 - 180.626)^2}{180.626}$$

$$+ \frac{(19 - 12.626)^2}{12.626} + \frac{(74 - 80.374)^2}{80.374}$$

$$= 5.38$$

$[\chi^2_{.05}(1) = 3.84]$

Reject H_0 and conclude that achievement level during high school varies as a function of performance during elementary school.

19-15 Study by Latané and Dabbs (1975) modified to 100 subjects/sex:

You can obtain the observed frequencies by multiplying the proportions times 100. Because this is a 2 x 2, we do not need to calculate expected frequencies.

	Female	Male	
Help	23	28	51
No Help	77	72	149
	100	100	200

$$\chi^2 = \frac{N(AD - BC)^2}{(A+B)(C+D)(A+C)(B+D)}$$

$$= \frac{200[(23)(72) - (28)(77)]^2}{(51)(149)(100)(100)}$$

$$= 0.658$$

$[\chi^2_{.05}(1) = 3.84]$

Do not reject H_0. Here we cannot reject H_0 because our χ^2 is too small.

19-16 With the smaller sample size, the power of the experiment was greatly reduced. The larger the sample size, the greater the power. Notice that the original example had a very large sample size.

19-18 The point of this question was to show that it is too easy to get carried away applying formulae and forgetting the question at hand. Although there may be no significant differences between the percentages, the fact that 45% of the students feel that the course needs major improvement is an important result. Simply comparing the data to an hypothesized 50:50 split, while tempting, is not a meaningful procedure for these data.

19-21 Faculty versus students on a basic statistical question:

First we need to convert percentages to number of "agree" and "disagree" responses with respect to the researcher. For example, 59% of 17 subjects is 10 subjects (round to a whole person).

(a) The researcher was correct. The probability of a Type I error does not depend on the size of the sample.

	Students	Asst. Prof.	Assoc. Prof.	Full Prof	
Agree	10 (7.40)	60 (76.13)	58 (58.30)	93 (79.18)	221
Disagree	7 (9.60)	115 (98.87)	76 (75.70)	89 (102.82)	287
	17	175	134	182	508

$$\chi^2 = \sum \frac{(O-E)^2}{E}$$

$$= \frac{(10-7.40)^2}{7.40} + \frac{(60-76.13)^2}{76.13} \cdots$$

$$\cdots + \frac{(76-75.70)^2}{75.70} + \frac{(89-102.82)^2}{102.82}$$

$$= 11.95$$

$[\chi^2_{.05}(3) = 7.82]$

Reject H_0.

(b)   There are significant differences among the groups of respondents in terms of their agreement or disagreement with the researcher. Since the researcher was correct, there are differences among the groups in terms of how likely they are to answer a simple statistical question correctly. In this case the students were more likely to be correct than the faculty, although we haven't run comparisons to test the statistical significance of that statement.

Chapter 20 - Distribution-free Tests

================================

20-1   Inferences in children's story summaries (McConaughy, 1980):

We first rank the data without regard to group, and then sum the ranks for each group.

(a) Analysis using the Mann-Whitney test (also known as Wilcoxon's rank-sum test):

Younger Children							Older Children					
Raw Data: 0	1	0	3	2	5	2	4	7	6	4	8	7
Ranks: 1.5	3	1.5	6	4.5	9	4.5	7.5	11.5	10	7.5	13	11.5

$\Sigma R = 30$ $N = 7$ $\qquad\qquad\qquad$ $\Sigma R = 61$ $N = 6$

$W_S = \Sigma R$ for group with smaller $N = 61$
$W_S' = 2\overline{W} - W_S = 84 - 61 = 23$

$W_S' < W_S$, therefore use W_S' in Appendix D. Double the probability level for a two-tailed test. By this I mean we look in the table at the column headed .025 for a two-tailed test at $\alpha = .05$.

$W_{.025}(6,7) = 27$

(b) Because 27 is greater than 23, reject H_0 and conclude that older children include more inferences in their summaries.

20-2   Amygdala lesions and fear responses (Kapp, Frysinger, Gallagher, & Hazelton, 1979):

(a) Analysis using the Mann-Whitney test:

Again we rank the data without regard to group and sum the ranks in each group.

Lesion	15	14	15	8	7	22	36	19	14	18	17
Ranks	14.5	12.5	14.5	7	6	19	20	18	12.5	17	16

Control	9	4	9	10	6	6	4	5	9
Ranks	9	1.5	9	11	4.5	4.5	1.5	3	9

$$W_S = 53 \quad W_S' = 2\overline{W} - W_S = 189 - 53 = 136$$

$W_S < W_S'$, therefore use W_S in Appendix D. Double the column probability level for a two-tailed test. Enter Table D.8 with $n_1 = 9$ and $n_2 = 11$ and look in the column headed .025. Here we find the entry of 68.

$$W_{.025}(9,11) = 68$$

(b) Because $68 > 53$, reject H_0 and conclude that subjects in the Lesion group take longer to learn the task, as the theory predicted. The lesion seems to reduce fear.

20-3 The analysis in Exercise 20-2 using the normal approximation:

Here we simply substitute the relevant values in the formula for z and find the probability of z from Appendix D.

$$z = \frac{W_S - \dfrac{n_1(n_1 + n_2 + 1)}{2}}{\sqrt{\dfrac{n_1 n_2(n_1 + n_2 + 1)}{12}}}$$

z	p
3.00	.0013
3.15	.0009
3.25	.0006

$$= \frac{53 - \dfrac{9(9 + 11 + 1)}{2}}{\sqrt{\dfrac{9 * 11(9 + 11 + 1)}{12}}}$$

$$= -3.15$$

Interpolate to get the probability and double that probability for a two-tailed test.

$$p(z \geq \pm 3.15) = 2(.0009) = .0018 < .05$$

Reject H_0, which was the same conclusion we came to in Exercise 20-2.

20-5 Hypothesis formation in psychiatric residents (Nurcombe & Fitzhenry-Coor, 1979):

Because we are using the same residents, the data are matched and we want Wilcoxon's match-pairs test. Find the differences, rank them, add signs to ranks, and sum positive and negative ranks.

(a) Analysis using Wilcoxon's matched-pairs signed-ranks test:

Before:	8	4	2	2	4	8	3	1	3	9
After:	7	9	3	6	3	10	6	7	8	7
Difference:	−1	+5	+1	+4	−1	+2	+3	+6	+5	−2
Rank:	2	8.5	2	7	2	4.5	6	10	8.5	4.5
Signed Rank:	−2	8.5	2	7	−2	4.5	6	10	8.5	−4.5

$T+ = \Sigma(\text{positive ranks}) = 46.5$

$T- = \Sigma(\text{negative ranks}) = 8.5$

$T = \text{smaller of } |T+| \text{ or } |T-| = 8.5$

$n = 10$

For $n = 10$ there are two entries; the probability of a sum less than 8 is .0244, and the probability of a sum less than 9 is .0322. We will have to double these for a two-tailed test, giving .0488 and .0644. If we want a two-tailed test with $p < .05$, we use 8 as the critical value.

$T_{.025}(10) = 8 < 8.5$ Do not reject H_0.

(b) We cannot conclude that we have evidence supporting the hypothesis that there is a reliable increase in hypothesis generation and testing over time. (Here is a case in which alternative methods of breaking ties could lead to different conclusions.)

20-8 The analysis in Exercise 20-7 using the normal approximation:

Here we simply substitute the relevant values in the formula for z.

$$z = \dfrac{T - \dfrac{n(n+1)}{4}}{\sqrt{\dfrac{n(n+1)(2n+1)}{24}}}$$

$$= \dfrac{46 - \dfrac{20(20+1)}{4}}{\sqrt{\dfrac{20(20+1)(2(20)+1)}{24}}} = -2.20$$

$p(z \geq \pm 2.20) = 2(.0139) = .0278 < .05$

Again reject H_0, which agrees with our earlier conclusion.

20-9   Data in Exercise 20-7 plotted as a function of firstborn's score:

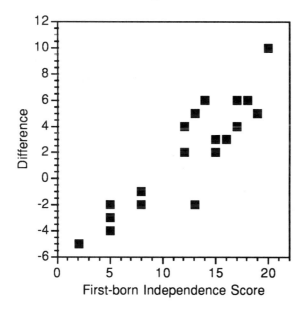

The scatter plots shows that the difference between the pairs is heavily dependent upon the score for the firstborn.

20-11 The Wilcoxon Matched-Pairs Signed-Ranks Test tests the null hypothesis that paired scores were drawn from identical populations or from

corresponding *t* test tests the null hypothesis that the paired scores were drawn from populations with the same mean and assumes normality.

20-12 The nature of the scale is important for the *interpretation* of the results but not for the choice of a statistical test on the actual numbers. For example, if two means or medians are different, then they are different. That does not mean that the difference is interpretable or meaningful.

20-14 Which professor has the best students?

This is an extension of the Mann-Whitney test in which we just rank the data in three groups instead of two.

Analysis using the Kruskal-Wallis oneway analysis of variance:

Professor A		Professor B		Professor C	
Score	Rank	Score	Rank	Score	Rank
82	21	55	3	65	9.5
71	15.5	88	24	54	2
56	4	85	23	66	11
58	5	83	22	68	12.5
63	7	71	15.5	72	17.5
64	8	70	14	78	20
62	6	68	12.5	65	9.5
53	1	72	17.5	73	19
R_i =	67.5		131.5		101

$N = 24 \quad n = 8$

$$H = \frac{12}{N(N+1)} \sum \frac{R_i^2}{n_i} - 3(N+1)$$

$$= \frac{12}{24(24+1)} \left[\frac{67.5^2}{8} + \frac{131.5^2}{8} + \frac{101^2}{8} \right] - 3(24+1)$$

$$= 5.124$$

We compare H to the chi-square distribution on $k - 1 = 2$ df. From the appendix, $\chi^2_{.05}(2) = 5.99$. Because our obtained value does not exceed 5.99, do not reject H_0.

20-16 Truancy of delinquents Before, During, and After placement in a group home:

These are repeated measurements, so we rank separately for each subject, and then sum the ranks in each group. It doesn't matter whether you rank from low to high, or vice versa.

Analysis using Friedman's test:

Before	During	After
10 (3)	5 (1)	8 (2)
12 (3)	8 (2)	7 (1)
12 (2)	13 (3)	10 (1)
19 (3)	10 (1)	12 (2)
5 (1)	10 (3)	8 (2)
13 (3)	8 (2)	7 (1)
20 (3)	16 (2)	12 (1)
8 (3)	4 (1)	5 (2)
12 (2)	14 (3)	9 (1)
10 (3)	3 (1)	5 (2)
8 (3)	3 (1.5)	3 (1.5)
18 (3)	16 (2)	2 (1)
(32)	(22.5)	(17.5)

$N = 12 \quad k = 3$

$$\chi^2_F = \frac{12}{Nk(k+1)}(\Sigma R_i^2) - 3N(k+1)$$

$$= \frac{12}{12(3)(3+1)}[32^2 + 22.5^2 + 17.5^2] - 3(12)(3+1)$$

$$= 9.042$$

We compare this result to the chi-square distribution on $k - 1 = 2$ df. $\chi^2_{.05}(2) = 5.99$. Since $9.042 > 5.99$, we can reject H_0 and conclude that truancy changed over time.

20-17 The study in Exercise 20-16 has the advantage over Exercise 20-15 in that it eliminates the influence of individual differences (differences in overall level of truancy from one person to another).

20-20 "The Mathematics of a Lady Tasting Tea.":

The title of these exercise came from a whimsical title that R. A. Fisher (1935)[1]

As in Exercise 12-16, we rank each person's ratings and then sum the ranks in each group.

First Cup	Second Cup	Third Cup
8 (3)	3 (2)	2 (1)
15 (3)	14 (2)	4 (1)
16 (2)	17 (3)	12 (1)
7 (3)	5 (2)	4 (1)
9 (3)	3 (1)	6 (2)
8 (2)	9 (3)	4 (1)
10 (3)	3 (1)	4 (2)
12 (3)	10 (2)	2 (1)
(22)	(16)	(10)

$N = 8 \quad k = 3$

$$\chi_F^2 = \frac{12}{Nk(k+1)}(\Sigma R_i^2) - 3N(k+1)$$

$$= \frac{12}{8(3)(3+1)}[22^2 + 16^2 + 10^2] - 3(8)(3+1)$$

$$= 9.00$$

We have $k = 3$ conditions, so we evaluate our result against the chi-square distribution on $3 - 1 = 2$ *df*. The critical value at $\alpha = .05$ is 5.99. Therefore we can reject the null hypothesis and conclude that people don't like tea made with used tea bags. Isn't science wonderful?

---

[1] Fisher, R. A. (1935) *The Design of Experiments*. Edinburgh: Oliver and Boyd.

Chapter 21 - Choosing the Appropriate Analysis

==

[N.B. Please review the disclaimer concerning these answers at the beginning of Chapter 21.]

21-1 This involves straight descriptive statistics, probably including boxplots of readability scores for items on each test. There are no hypotheses to be tested.

21-3 They would use Pearson's r to correlate Denver test scores and scores on individually administered intellectual measures. The question might be taken to imply that some children's scores were based on one measure of intelligence and the rest of the children's scores were based on a different measure. In this case you could sort the children into groups and compute correlations for each group. In either case, it would be sensible to make a scatterplot of the data and examine the linearity of the relationship.

21-4 They presumably want to ask if people recognize pictures they have seen better than pictures they have not seen. They could run a t test for two independent groups to compare the two group means. They could then obtain the correlation between the percent-correct score and the reported level of use of study aids. (You should recall that with two groups, a t test and a one-way analysis of variance are equivalent tests.)

21-6 There are two independent variables in this design (Type of Cue During Learning versus Type of Cue During Recall), and we want to compare means. This is a 2 x 3 analysis of variance.

21-7 Here we have three groups differing in prior experience. We want to compare their means on speed of learning. This is a one-way analysis of variance.They could also use protected t tests to compare individual groups, if that is necessary.

21-9 Here we have two independent groups with three different dependent variables. The author could run three separate t tests for independent groups, but might want to use a more stringent level of significant, e.g. $\alpha = .01$, to avoid a high familywise error rate.

21-10 This is a more complex repeated-measures analysis of variance than the one we considered in Chapter 18. It is a 2 x 2 factorial design with Good versus Poor Readers and Easy versus Difficult Passages as the factors. Reader is a between-subject variable (different people are in the two groups), and Passages is a within-subject variable (the same people read both kinds of passages).

21-12 They should compare the two groups on locus of control scores, and maybe on Peabody scores, using t tests for independent samples. They could also correlate Nowicki-Strickland and Peabody using Pearson's r. The Peabody scores allow us to check on whether locus of control varies with intelligence, and whether the two groups show differences in intelligence (which may reflect how well they take tests rather than their intelligence).

21-13 The authors simply want to compare the performance of three groups. They could use a one-way analysis of variance on the MFFT score for the second administration. They should probably also run it on the scores for the first administration to check the experimental hypothesis that the groups started out together. (A more complex repeated-measures design also would be suitable [see Exercise 21-10], but I'd be inclined to stick with the two one-way analyses because of their ease of interpretation.)

21-14 Each subject tasted all juices, so this is a repeated-measures analysis of variance comparing the four flavors. The corresponding distribution-free test would be Friedman's rank test, where we would rank the flavors separately for each judge.

21-16 **(a)** He should run a 2 x 2 (Group by Abstinent versus Smoking) chi-square test at each time interval. We cannot make Interval a third variable in this analysis because the same subjects were involved at each interval. **(b)** We don't know whether the nicotine in the gum had any effect. It might be that chewing any kind of gum was the controlling factor.

21-17 This is a difficult one, partly because it depends on what Payne wants to know. I assume she wants to know how rankings of characteristics agree across sexes or across years. She could first find the mean rank assigned to each characteristic separately for each sex and year. Because the raw data were originally ranks, I would probably be inclined to then rank these mean values. She could then calculate Spearman's r_S between males and females for each year or between years within each sex. The correlations would be obtained for the 10 pairs of scores (one pair per characteristic).

21-18 The samples for each distance are paired because each subject has a score under each distance. They should use a t test for two related samples. If they don't want to use a parametric test, they should use the Wilcoxon matched-pairs signed-ranks test.

21-19 There are two independent groups in this experiment. The authors should use a Mann-Whitney test to compare average locus of control scores.

21-20 They should use a t test for related samples—the samples are related because Smith and Plant formed matched pairs. They would run tests on each satisfaction area. (They could also use a complex repeated-measures analysis with "area" as another independent variable.)

21-21 They should begin with a 2 x 3 chi-square test for the contingency table formed by Correct vs Incorrect identification and Group Membership. The cells would contain the frequencies of correct and incorrect identification. They could then follow this up with a oneway analysis of variance on the three groups' confidence scores. Assuming that the F is significant, they could follow this up with a protected t test, comparing the two "theft" conditions.

21-22 This is a situation for a chi-square goodness-of-fit test. The conditions are Rotated vs. Stationary, and the count is the number of subjects choosing that condition as giving stronger contours. The expected values would be $37/2 = 18.5$.

21-24 This is another complex repeated-measures analysis of variance. The comparison of recall of the two lists (one learned before administration of the drug and the other learned after) is a repeated measurement because the same subjects are involved. The comparison of the drug versus saline groups is a between-subjects effect because the groups involve different subjects.

21-25 This is a t test for two independent groups, because we have different subjects in the two groups and we want to compare the group means on sleepiness.

21-26 We have three independent groups, and the dependent variable for each subject was the number of errors out of the 12 faces presented. The authors could use the Kruskal-Wallis test to compare the three groups and, if that was significant, use the Mann-Whitney test to compare individual groups the way they would otherwise have used a protected t test.